THE
FRONTIER ROMANCE

ENVIRONMENT, CULTURE, AND ALASKA IDENTITY

Judith Kleinfeld

University of Alaska Press
Fairbanks

University of Alaska Press
P.O. Box 756240
Fairbanks, AK 99775-6240

ISBN 978-1-60223-189-4 (paper)
ISBN 978-1-60223-190-0 (electronic)

Library of Congress Cataloging-in-Publication Data

Kleinfeld, Judith.
    The frontier romance : environment, culture, and Alaska identity / by Judith
Kleinfeld.
        p. cm.
    Includes bibliographical references and index.
    ISBN 978-1-60223-189-4 (alk. paper) — ISBN 978-1-60223-190-0 (electronic)
1. Alaska—Description and travel. 2. Alaska—Social life and culture. 3. Frontier
and pioneer life—Alaska—Psychological aspects. 4. Community life—Alaska—Case
studies. I. Title.
    F910.5.K54 2012
    979.8—dc23
        2012005520

Cover design by Kristina Kachele
Cover photo ©2012 Kevin G. Smith/AlaskaStock.com

This publication was printed on acid-free paper that meets the minimum
requirements for ANSI / NISO Z39.48–1992 (R2002) (Permanence of Paper for
Printed Library Materials).

Printed in the United States

Contents

Introduction:
How Literature Turns into Life

I cannot imagine a more important psychological research
project than one that addresses itself to the "development of
autobiography"—how our way of telling about ourselves changes and
how these accounts come to take control of our ways of life.

—Jerome Bruner, "Life as Narrative." *Social
Research*, 54, no. 1 (spring 1987)

To travel to Alaska is to enter an American storybook, a land where mountain men still seek freedom in the forest, pioneer families still homestead in the wilderness, and spiritual seekers still build, with the labor of their own hands, a "city on a hill" in a barren land. Why do people turn their backs on the comforts and conveniences the modern world offers and choose to live such strange and difficult lives? And why do such journeys into the wilderness still quicken our pulse and thrill our hearts?

When I first asked these questions, I was on a quest of my own, to document the lives of these hidden people before they disappeared into history. Alaska still styles itself as "The Last Frontier," but the state is fast becoming the "lost frontier." The end of homesteading and new environmental regulations that designated lands formerly used for habitation as wilderness areas and wildlife refuges make it more and more difficult for people to find a piece of wilderness and live out America's frontier story. Not only the opportunity but also the impulse to live in the wilderness is disappearing. Many of the wilderness dwellers who came to Alaska were part of a generational moment—the seekers of the sixties who rejected what they saw as materialistic lives and sought alternative lives that honored the natural world. But Alaska's wilderness dwellers are still here, if you know where to find them.

The wilderness dwellers in Alaska are living out a powerful cultural narrative, America's frontier romance. The narrative celebrates the migration story of Americans, the way so many of our ancestors left home in search of a better life. It celebrates courage and self-reliance and the search for freedom.

This book describes the ways in which America's foundational epic, the frontier romance, shapes the plot lines of so many of our lives. When I interviewed the hidden people in the wilderness about why they had come to Alaska, most described the influence of film and storybooks—especially heroic films like *Jeremiah Johnson*, childhood stories about Daniel Boone and Davy Crockett, and, in the case of frontier women, *Little House on the Prairie*. Few studies show how this happens, how the master narratives of a culture give birth to lives. It makes a difference what stories a culture celebrates, frontier stories or warrior stories, trickster stories or martyrdom stories.

This book makes these points: (1) cultural stories shape people's lives; (2) Alaska offers vivid, contemporary illustrations of America's shared story, the frontier romance; and (3) America's frontier romance provides cultural scaffolding for freedom, helping us to be a people who savor the experience of freedom rather than fearing it.

The Frontier Romance

What I call the "frontier romance" is what historians call the "West of the imagination."[1] This West of the imagination was an "uncomplicated, sparsely populated area characterized by noble and distinctive individuals, personified by mountain men, trappers, cowboys, and hardy pioneer farmers. Its symbols, such as the log cabin, are instantly recognizable by people of every background, fraught with emotion and shared cultural values." This is not the actual West but rather the West as a set of symbols, images, and myths. After the Civil War, when Americans were searching for a unifying national identity, the idea took hold that "westering" defined the American experience and depicted the American character. The idea was played out in popular culture through Buffalo Bill's immensely popular Wild West shows, through Frederic Remington's cowboy paintings and sculptures, through Owen Wister's novel *The Virginian: A Horseman of the Plains*. Frederick Jackson Turner's 1893 essay, "The Significance of the Frontier in American History," developed the idea of the westward expansion as the single most important influence on the character of the nation and the crucible creating the American character: "To the frontier the American intellect owes its striking characteristics, that coarseness and strength combined with acuteness and inquisitiveness, that practical, inventive turn of mind, quick to find expedients; that masterful grasp of material things, lacking in the artistic but powerful to effect great ends; that restless, nervous energy; that dominant individualism, working for good and for evil, and withal that buoyancy and exuberance which comes with freedom. These are the traits of the frontier, or traits called out elsewhere because of the existence of the frontier."[2]

Yale historian John Mack Faragher calls Turner's essay "the single most influential piece of writing in the history of American history."[3] Historians would debate Turner's idea of the frontier for over a century, first elaborating it, then critiquing it, then attacking it with the energy and vitriol of an ideological crusade. The frontier was not America's triumph but its shame, argued the New Western historians of the 1980s, describing the racism, disrespect for women, violence, and environmental desecration of the western movement.[4] Yet the idea that the frontier had somehow shaped the nation and its character would not die and be decently buried even after academic historians in books and journal articles had performed the last rites. Popular culture still celebrates the earlier notion of the American frontier, as in Walt Disney World's "Frontierland" or the memorable message of *Star Trek* "to boldly go where no man has gone before." Turner's frontier thesis, though riddled with historical errors, still defines the American mythos.

America's frontier romance is what narrative psychologists call a "master narrative," a ritualized story that moves through many imaginative forms—history, literature, art, advertising, film, and television. The basic story line follows a three-part pattern. The hero leaves the security of home, together with the safety and the shackles of his birthplace. The hero goes out into the wilderness, into a world strange and new, facing danger, tests, and trials, in a great quest. In this crucible of adversity, the hero forges a better self and returns to forge a better world. The frontier romance displays and celebrates what Americans consider to be their defining national virtues—an instinctive love of freedom, individualism, and self-reliance. But the frontier romance creates more than a character ideal and more than a moral order. The story also creates a distinctive emotional experience, which, I will argue later, is crucial to the unrecognized cultural and psychological functions the story serves—providing emotional support for the experience of freedom, of venturing out into the unknown.

While the western frontier hero is the creation of the American imagination, its lineage is far more ancient. The western hero is the American variant of *The Hero with a Thousand Faces* what Joseph Campbell calls the "monomyth."[5] The hero narrative follows a uniform pattern across different times and cultures. Campbell offers the most influential description of this heroic life pattern in its cultural variations. The hero—Jesus, Buddha, Achilles, Oedipus—departs from his community; undertakes a journey into the unknown; faces and overcomes ordeals, tests, and trials; and returns with a life-transmuting trophy or a regenerative message for his society. In some versions of the narrative, the hero perishes, like Phaeton, born of a virgin in Ethiopia, who sets off across Persia and India to find the palace of the Sun, only to crash and burn when he drives his solar chariot too near the sun. Without genuine risk, the heroic quest would have no meaning.

The distinctive contribution of the frontier romance, the American version of the heroic monomyth, is to *democratize* the hero's journey. In its classic versions, the hero is a young man of noble parentage or special birth. In the American frontier romance, the hero is everyman or everywoman. The hero can be nothing more than a scamp, like Huckleberry Finn, floating down the Mississippi River on a raft, who reckoned he was going to "set out for the territories ahead of all the rest." The Klondike quest, the migration West, embraced the restless and ambitious from every station of life.

The frontier romance, America's epic narrative, creates what mythologists call a "cosmos," a map that orders both the physical and the moral world.[6] The geographic and spiritual cosmos of the frontier romance is "the newness, the vastness, the openness, of America—the freedom thereby granted Americans. [It is] the epic of the forests, the prairies, the plains. It is the epic of discoverers, explorers, pioneers, of Columbus, Daniel Boone, and Lewis and Clark, of the Oregon trail, the Mormon trek, the transcontinental railway."[7] What beckons the cultural inhabitants of the frontier cosmos is the journey of exploration and enterprise, the journey to uncharted regions.

This moral cosmos is so familiar to us that most of us do not realize that this concept of the frontier is not a given. This conception of the frontier as an inviting realm of possibility was born in America.[8] The original meaning of *frontier* was a border or a boundary, the very opposite of its Americanized meaning of inviting possibility. *Frontier* in the European sense means a *boundary*, not an open space, a *limit*, not a beckoning place. In French, for example, the word *frontiére* means simply the border and figuratively implies a boundary. In Mandarin Chinese, the most common dictionary term for *frontier* is "bian jie," meaning "boundary." In Cantonese, the word for *frontier* is "huang die," which carries negative connotations. In the Chinese cultural cosmos, one does not set out for the frontier, one is sent to the frontier, a place of punishment and exile, a wilderness as wasteland. During the American expansion west, the meaning of the word *frontier* was turned on its head, its dominant definition changing from its European meaning of "border" and "boundary" to its American meaning of "openness" and "possibility." The *Australian National Dictionary* and the *Western Canadian Dictionary and Phrasebook*, for example, explicitly label this positive meaning of the word *frontier* an "Americanism." We construct in our imagination frontiers in any realm that offers challenge and the excitement of the new. Homebodies who never leave their computers "homestead the electronic frontier." Retirement we call the "next frontier." Even selling panties turns into a pioneer drama as in this amusing newspaper headline: "Fashion's New Frontier: Racy Lingerie for the Larger-Size Woman."

What are the psychological effects of this pervasive American symbol system, of so many stock characters, from the cowboy and mountain man of the West to the space explorer voyaging to the unknown regions of the solar system? And what cultural functions does this frontier romance serve?

The frontier romance, this study argues, is a crucial psychological support in a culture that celebrates freedom as its central, signature value. The frontier romance creates psychological scaffolding that enables people to bear the burdens of freedom. That we assume a love of freedom is "natural" in itself attests to the triumph of our cultural narrative and its symbol system.[9] To leave the comfort and security of home and go out into the wilderness in search of a better life and a better world is far from natural, as Tocqueville observed in his journey through America in 1831. His provocative observations occur after his travels to the American frontier, then located in the remote region of Michigan. Later, in August 1831, he journeys to Canada, where he encounters the French-Canadians, a people he immediately admires, who remind him of home, the people of his heart.[10] But Tocqueville is distressed that the French he encounters, unlike the Americans, are not moving west and extending French influence and empire. Why not? The French in the New World have the same opportunities. As the able and respected French-Canadian John Neilson informs him, the French do not choose to advance west in Canada even though "there is to be found some excellent land, that is almost always given away for almost nothing and that can easily be put into cultivation."[11] Disturbed by this news, Tocqueville makes pointed inquiries and concludes in his diary that the French prefer to stay within the security of their towns and enjoy the delights of communal life: "There is gathered four times a day about a round table a family composed of vigorous parents and buxom, merry children. After supper one sings some old French *chanson*."[12] Why would they leave the joy of family and the gaiety of life at home to live in isolated log cabins?

To take pleasure in freedom, to revel in risk, rather than to take pleasure in security, is the spiritual message of the American frontier romance. This is a story Americans live by, not only during the expansion west, but in everyday life. Take a look at the self-help shelf of Barnes and Noble or Amazon.com, with book after book exhorting us to "break free" from whatever is holding us back, to take the risk of leaving our old lives behind, to explore not only new worlds but also our inner worlds. We are exhorted not to "let fear of the unknown sabotage our success."

From the unfree state of much of the world, it is obvious that freedom does not come easily. Most Americans consider freedom a blessing, a universal good, which it is their special mission to bring to other countries. But those psychologists who have studied the psychological experience of freedom emphasize freedom's burdens. Barry Schwartz argues that freedom, which he defines as a multiplicity of choices, creates anxiety and actually reduces life satisfaction.[13] In *Escape from Freedom*, Erich Fromm suggests freedom is a psychological problem.[14] Writing in 1941, during the rise of the Nazi regime, he asks why modern man is "tempted to surrender his freedom to dictators of all kinds."[15]

Coercive regimes and tradition-saturated cultures have continuing appeal, Fromm argues, because freedom brings with it serious psychological burdens. In the medieval world, despite its constraints, people felt emotionally safe and secure. The breakdown of feudalism brought in the Renaissance "an increased feeling of strength" but with it as well "an increased isolation, doubt, skepticism, and—resulting from all these— anxiety."[16] Freedom is a lonely state of mind. We can no longer rest sweetly in the cradle of convention, our lives marked out in clear paths before us. With freedom comes unparalleled personal choice but also the burden of making choices.

Perhaps the sharpest pain of freedom, in a society that values individual achievement very highly, is the pain of "no excuses." In an America with presumably no limits, you have no one but yourself to blame if you fail. And no matter how great your achievement, you could always have accomplished more. Freedom bangs us up against the wall of our own limitations.

That Americans embrace freedom rather than seeking to escape it, that Americans define the experience of freedom as a supreme pleasure, comes from many sources, but one of the most influential is our shared cultural narrative, the frontier romance. We Americans romance ourselves into frontiers everywhere, not just the frontiers of Davy Crockett, Daniel Boone, John Wayne, and Jack London. Leveraged buyout specialists who have never touched a gun are termed "gunslingers" in *Barron's* financial weekly. We push ourselves toward risk and accomplishment by reminding ourselves "no guts, no glory."

The frontier and its freedom, however, is not an entirely positive concept. Critics point out that the concept of frontier has been used to justify environmental despoliation and rapacious destruction of public resources for personal gain. Unfettered freedom means the strong exploiting the weak. Due to gender and race, privileged groups have freedom at the expense of others.

To understand the influence of the frontier romance on people's lives and the psychological and cultural functions of this narrative, I explore in this study the life histories of people who have chosen to go to Alaska, to a state that labels itself "The Last Frontier" and "The Last Great Wilderness." Many question whether Alaska is still frontier. In *Coming into the Country*, for example, John McPhee characterizes Anchorage, where most Alaskans live, as "an American spore. A large cookie cutter brought down on El Paso could lift something like Anchorage into the air. Anchorage is the northern rim of Trenton. . . . It is condensed, instant Albuquerque."[17]

Despite this cynicism, the frontier mythology is still important in its inhabitants' imaginations. Despite the big-box stores, fast-food restaurants, and suburban developments of Alaska's cities, those who wish to see a frontier in Alaska can find in actuality the symbols they seek—log cabins, gold mines, people hunting and fishing for food, and stock frontier characters, like trappers and miners with long, grizzled beards wearing Carhartt overalls and faded flannel shirts who swagger as they walk. Historians of the West marvel at how people can project a frontier onto the West or such a place as Alaska, when the reality of the scene—cities, sidewalks, big box stores—have nothing to do with the historical frontier. But even in the twenty-first century, a statewide survey showed that over ninety percent of the population strongly agreed that "Alaska is still the Last Frontier," and over eighty percent strongly agreed that, in Alaska, "people have more opportunities to do and be what they want."[18]

While Alaska's nickname of "The Last Frontier" is in part a tourist ploy, the state does qualify, in a literal sense, as a frontier region. The census definition of "frontier" is a geographic region of fewer than two people per square mile, and Alaska has 1.9 people per square mile. Most of Alaska's population of around 670,000 people is clustered in Anchorage and its environs. To find people who see themselves as living on the frontier, one must leave Alaska's cities and go to more remote regions, such as the small towns scattered in the interior of Alaska or the cabins in the wilderness. These regions of Alaska offer the staging for the frontier romance—rivers, rapids, and mountains; moose, caribou, and grizzly bears; Eskimo and Indian villages; and remote wilderness where, in some places, no human footstep has ever fallen.

But this frontier is constructed in the imagination and personally created on the ground through such activities as building log cabins in the wilderness and hunting for meat. What is romance and what is reality is an issue that these wilderness dwellers themselves puzzle about. Like Buffalo Bill, an actual buffalo hunter who donned a fancy costume and played himself in the fabulous Wild West shows of the early twentieth century, these Alaska frontier dwellers have gone into the actual wilderness and at the same time donned the wilderness personas of characters from literature and film. The story and the reality weave together like the threads creating the heroic scenes in a medieval tapestry.

Methods

The lives of people who go to Alaska and live out, in a literal way, America's epic frontier romance, offer an opportunity to understand how stories shape people's lives. This research took place over a ten-year period during which I first recorded the life histories of and studied through the methods of participant observation seventy-five people who had migrated to Alaska and incorporated into their lives obvious frontier symbols. They built log cabins in the wilderness, hunted or fished for much of their food, or lived on traplines like nineteenth-century mountain men. Some lived more conventional city lives, but they narrated their lives as people who had come to Alaska to find a frontier. Each open-ended interview lasted from one to three hours, was tape-recorded, and then analyzed for central themes and images. The interview began with the question, "Why did you come to Alaska?" and continued with questions on experiences in Alaska and how living in Alaska had influenced them. For many people, the decision to go to and stay in Alaska was a central turning point in their lives. Each interview concluded with a question that provoked a pause in the conversation and proved to be the most revealing, "What do you think the story of your life should say?"

I also conducted case studies, over a period of several years, of two frontier communities: (1) a community of self-styled "pioneer women" who lived in the remote town of Central, close to the Yukon River, and (2) a community of spiritual seekers who lived in a communal society that they had built themselves in the wilderness, a contemporary version of the intentional communities scattered throughout nineteenth-century frontier America, where groups of people could acquire cheap land.

Drafts of the chapters were sent to the communities and key informants for review and correction of errors. To my surprise, many people did not want the anonymity and confidentiality conventional in social research. They wanted me to use their actual names. They saw their unconventional lives as a personal achievement and wanted author's credit for the story of their lives. Nonetheless, following the conventions of social science research, I often use pseudonyms. In these cases, I place in quotation marks the first use of their names.

The central theme of this project—the influence of the American frontier romance on people's lives—developed as the research progressed. I did not begin with the question of how stories shaped lives. Rather, I became intrigued with how often people talked about childhood stories, films, and historical narratives when I asked the question, "Why did you come to Alaska?" Some told family stories, such as the cherished tale of an ancestor who had come over on the *Mayflower* or who had gone west in a covered wagon. They saw themselves as the protagonists in similar heroic stories, with the tales coming from a vast array of narrative forms—historical reading, adventure stories, and family history.

The Contribution of This Study to Narrative Psychology

The narrative study of lives has become an influential movement throughout the social sciences. The "narrative turn" encompasses a diversity of epistemologies—case studies, autobiography, ethnographies, discourse analysis, and other hermeneutic strategies of inquiry. In common is an emphasis on lived meaning, on the ways in which people use narrative to create a sense of self. The unifying idea is this: the self is not some inner essence to be discovered. The self is created through narrative and altered for different audiences, including ourselves.

Narrative psychology has made a valuable practical contribution, not only to psychological theory but also to therapy.[19] What needs doctoring, from this theoretical perspective, is not the patient but the patient's story. The task for the therapist is to co-author with the patient a new life story, a "healing plot." The patient may tell, for example, a victim story and the therapist helps create an agentic story that re-narrates the past and provides a life script for moving forward. Therapy provides a site where people can seek, through narrative, help in dealing with the problems posed by freedom, the complex and ambiguous choices that are both blessing and burden. This study shows how some wilderness dwellers use a frontier persona as a source of self-therapy. They use the master narrative of the frontier romance to give themselves an honored identity while they escape into the wilderness to recover. For others, the frontier narrative becomes a mask and disguise. While they claim an honorable identity, they wreak havoc on their families and the wilderness communities in which they have taken refuge.

The contribution of this research is to show not how people use story to interpret their lives—after the fact—but rather how people use stories such as the frontier romance to direct their lives; how stories drive decisions and spur action; one contribution of this research is to show how the same master narrative can take a variety of forms and serve diverse psychological functions. The frontier romance can drive both conventional ambition, as in Horace Greeley's exhortation to "go west, young man, and grow up with the country," and also rebellion from conventional ambition, as in Henry David Thoreau's celebration of those who "hear the music of a different drummer."

While narrative psychologists have given attention to the way people draw from cultural themes in creating their own life narratives, master narratives in themselves have received little scholarly attention. An important exception is Dan McAdams' study of the "redemptive self."[20] The redemptive story provides narrative guidelines for creating meaning from suffering. Highly generative middle-aged adults, McAdams finds,

tend to tell stories about their lives that follow the redemptive plot out-
line. The story begins with a main character who enjoys some special
blessing or advantage. Along with the hero's experiencing an early advantage in life is the parallel theme of an early sensitivity to the suffering
of others, leading to an implicit message, "I am blessed, but others suffer."
The plot develops with the character encountering obstacles and setbacks
but rising from adversity. The story ends with the protagonist working for
the well-being of others, turning his own suffering into a legacy for humanity. The redemption narrative promotes growth and good works but,
McAdams points out, has its dark side. The story line includes the glib
idea that we can expect deliverance from suffering and a naive refusal
to recognize the tragic dimension of life—some acts are evil and cannot
be redeemed.

The Plot Elements of the Frontier Romance

The frontier romance is most often a coming-of-age story, a story of
youth, of setting out into the world. The frontier romance, however, is
also about bravery—having the courage to leave an old life behind and
begin again in a new world.[21]

HOW DOES THE STORY BEGIN?

The hero of the tale is stuck in a trap, caught up in the rat race, facing a
lifetime of convention and constraint. The hero usually sees himself as
a maverick, someone who does not fit into the society of his birth, and
literature is often the path to liberation. The following story illustrates
these themes in the people I interviewed.

> "Vincent" knew by the time he was ten years old that he wanted out
> of his Italian neighborhood in Brooklyn. His brother had wound up
> serving time on Rikers Island. Even if he stayed straight, he saw his life
> laid out before him from his birth to his death. In his Italian neighbor-
> hood, first the parents lived downstairs and their newly married chil-
> dren lived upstairs. When the babies came, the young adults moved
> downstairs and the old folks moved upstairs.

A book by Terris Moore, *Mount McKinley: The Pioneer Climbs*, gave Vincent a vision of a pure new world where giants still walked the earth. Vincent imagined himself as a "giant fountain pen" composing a new life story for himself on the clean white snow. When he turned eighteen, he took off for the University of Alaska, where he lived in Moore Hall, named after his hero Terris Moore. He climbed to the top of Mount McKinley and climbed to the top of his company.

When Terris Moore was dying, Vincent called him to let him know that his book on exploration had given him a vision for a new life. "Terris literally cried, he cried hard, and so did his wife, Katrina," Vincent said. "I cried, too, thinking about the impact his book on pioneering had on a kid from Brooklyn."

HOW DOES THE STORY DEVELOP?

The hero enters into the second phase of the heroic journey, what Campbell calls "the road of trials." A supernatural figure or some other wise helper often provides the young adventurer with aid on this perilous journey. "Yes, you are an untried youngster moving among powerful, experienced people, some of them malevolent," the wise helper says, "but you are young, brave, and pure of heart. Take the risk. You are sufficient." The hero accepts the risk and discovers talents he never knew he possessed and develops abilities he never knew he had.

Before "Alison" came to Alaska, she was wandering homeless on the beach, her legs swollen with bug bites. She came to Alaska to be with her boyfriend, and the frontier ethos started to shape her life. Her journalism professor, Claudia Clark, saw much raw talent in Alison and became her helper and guide, with tough messages about what she could do if she only wanted to.

In Alaska, Alison became the morning news anchor, the gal who got the crime footage, who did the exotic stories about oil in Prudhoe Bay and the Midnight Sun baseball game. She did amusing news, like the wandering dog in the tiny town of Cordova that cab drivers took home when he got loose. Big news outlets such as CNN often picked up Alaska stories.

In Alaska, she got noticed. If Alison didn't get up before dawn and film that fire, people weren't going to see footage of the blaze. Alaska became her trampoline, catapulting Alison to the Columbia School of Journalism and then to ABC News. Where she came from, Pueblo, Colorado, she was limited by her past: A daughter of a prominent family, she had dropped out of college, had been hospitalized for depression, and had become a beach bum. In Alaska, Alison turned into a TV personality and developed the confidence to leave Alaska for New York and big-time broadcasting.

HOW DOES THE STORY END?

In the classic hero narrative, the main character returns home with a life-regenerating message or trophy. But the community may refuse this gift of renewal. The return is what Campbell calls the hero's "ultimate difficult task." The hero must figure out how to teach again "what has been taught correctly and incorrectly learned a thousand thousand times, throughout the millenniums of mankind's prudent folly."

Pam and Jeff Haskin left their thriving taxidermy business in Arizona and went off to homestead outside of Central, Alaska. To get title to their land, they had to live on the land for twenty-five months over five years. To build a cabin, they chopped down trees and peeled off the bark. They melted snow for water, dug a hole and built their outhouse.

"We were on our way to success in life, but we wanted more from life than a thirty-year mortgage and a new car in the driveway. We didn't want to get to the end of our lives and say, "Well, we really had a nice house and we drove a new car all the time."

Pam developed a dream of becoming a professional writer and *Guideposts* started publishing her stories about the tests of courage and character she faced in the wilderness. In *A Deliberate Life*, her account of homesteading in Alaska at the end of the twentieth century, she casts her life as a parable of the spirit. She sees herself as "lighting a candle."

"You do not need to accept the little life you are born into," she tells high school students when she is asked to speak about her life as a homesteader in the Alaska wilderness. "You too can choose how to live. You too can break with the past. You too can live your dream."

How the Frontier Narrative Weaves Romance with Reality

The focus of this study is on the frontier narrative as a story, a set of images and symbols that shape an individual's construction of reality. But I do not mean to suggest that the frontier is nothing but a figment of the imagination. Quite the contrary, Alaska and other frontier societies, whether they exist in a geographic space or in a metaphoric realm, present sociological actualities:

1. Frontiers are underpopulated settings where people enjoy easier entry, less competition, and better odds of success.
2. Frontiers are strange and new to those who come and this atmosphere enlivens perceptions, imagination, and creativity.
3. Frontiers are cultural crossroads where people of different backgrounds come together in a new and turbulent society with unsettled institutions and a less formed social hierarchy.
4. Frontiers create genuine dangers, and this knowledge makes the test and quest have meaning.

Astute observers see these societal differences. Deciding whether to leave settled Baltimore for the raw city of the nineteenth-century Chicago, historian Herbert Baxter Adams listed the pros and cons of a settled setting versus a society in ferment:[22]

Baltimore	*Chicago*
Quiet	Rush
Continuity	Broken
Experience	Experiment
Society	New People
Conservatism	Boom
Duty	Advantage
Assured Position	All New
Settled	Moving
Identification	Lost

Living in a frontier society with these characteristics, however, does not mean that people will see and use these opportunities. Many people who come to Alaska see nothing but ordinary American towns, no different from anyplace else. They approach this new world not through the frontier romance but through small-town American boosterism, the view expressed in the lyrics of Rodgers and Hammerstein's stage show *Oklahoma*: "Everything's up to date in Kansas City/They gone about as fer as they can go/They went an' built a skyscraper seven stories high/About as high as a buildin' orta grow." Other people come to Alaska and see the American frontier, with its spectacular wilderness, indigenous Eskimos and Indians, and wild and dangerous beauty. The frontier romance provides a script—with stock scenes, costumes, plot lines, themes, and attitudes—that people project onto the stage.

The Psychological Functions of the Frontier Romance

In this book, I describe people who came to Alaska to live out different versions of the frontier romance. I omit the most common version of the story, the "go west, young man" usage of the frontier romance to drive ambition and seek new opportunity, since the psychological function of this story—setting off to new territory to rise in the world—is well-known.

The first chapter tells the story of the modern-day mountain men who trap for fur in Alaska's interior forests. The pursuit rarely pays enough to support them. They trap for other purposes. They see themselves as bearing witness to lost American values of independence and self-sufficiency. Their lives offer living testimony that, even in the modern world, a man can live free. They use the frontier romance as a way of proving up, of achieving and validating manhood.

Chapter 2 tells the story of pioneer women who have settled in a remote Alaska town where they have re-created in their imaginations and on the ground a pioneer community celebrating traditional American virtues of self-reliance and community. Within the public narrative are individual frontier narratives—stories of redemption and rebirth, stories of rebellion against materialist values, and love stories of two intertwined lives with the wilderness becoming a metaphor for the dangers and difficulties of life faced together. From the perspective of narrative psychology, a special contribution of this chapter is the emphasis on the ironic enactment of a story. A second contribution of this chapter is the way the women weave together as a group a heroic story of their lives for public consumption, while their private stories are different, involving conflicts such as their worry about following a man rather than living out the narrative of a self-sufficient modern woman.

The third chapter tells the story of odd and, in some cases, dangerous characters, psychologically disturbed men who disguise themselves through the frontier romance. They use its imagery to create a persona that in their own eyes and in the eyes of their audience gives them respect. For some, the frontier romance functions as a healing narrative. The story serves as self-medication, turning messy lives into works of art. In other cases, their psychological disturbance breaks out of their frontier costumes, and they wreak destruction. One case describes a mass murderer who hides out as a "mountain man." Another case describes a sexual predator who lives out the fantasy of a pioneer family in the wilderness with his wife and fifteen children until jailed for incest. This chapter explores the use of a story as a mask, using the frontier romance to hide psychopathology and to deceive communities accustomed to frontier adventurers.

The fourth chapter describes the use of narrative to drive not individual lives but rather the group life of a community. I tell the story of modern-day pilgrims, the people of Whitestone Farms who caravanned across America to create in Alaska a city on a hill where they can live in community, sharing all they produce. They build with the labor of their own hands a city in the wilderness, where they can separate themselves from the spiritual barrenness they see in contemporary America. Their community is an amalgam of different stories: the first Christians who shared all they had, stories of rebirth and redemption, and the frontier romance. Like the classical heroes whose lives communicate a rejuvenating message, the community of Whitestone Farms also affects many people who experience its ethos. Those who come find a world of the spirit and a frontier of the spirit that they did not realize even existed. I count myself among them.

The conclusion describes how the frontier romance can shape not only such extreme, exotic lives but also a moment in an ordinary life.

On a drive home from the office, a lawyer, a "suit," enters into and enacts the frontier romance, complete with its costumes and props, its heroic imagery, and its ethical message. The frontier narrative leaps into life, creating a fantastic episode, which the lawyer turns the next day into an entertaining narrative for his colleagues and his family. But the story also communicates a lesson of moral action.

The frontier narrative is one of America's cultural treasures, creating the psychological scaffolding for freedom. It is a narrative that fuels both conventional ambition and rebellion from convention. It is a narrative that tells us how much freedom we have if only we will use it. It is a narrative that tells us to live deliberately, to gather our courage and take the risk, to face the danger, to seize freedom rather than fear it, and to feel the rush of the wind in our hair.

CHAPTER 1

······································

Modern-Day Mountain Men

But he was a man. He possessed the most formidable skill ever developed on this continent. He possessed too, a valor hardly to be contemplated. He went forth into the uncharted peaks and made his way.

—Bernard DeVoto, quoted in *Mountain Man: A Novel of Male and Female in the Early American West*, by Vardis Fisher (Mattituck, NY: Aeonian Press, 1977)

In the Alaska wilderness roam trappers whose lives recall the legendary mountain men who trapped beaver in Rocky Mountain streams, the men who explored and opened up the Far West. The mountain man's day of glory was brief but left a long legacy in fable and story. The Rocky Mountain Fur Company, founded in 1822, pioneered a revolutionary approach to taking beaver, sending out trappers to take fur in the winter, when pelts were at their peak. The mountain men symbolized independence and self-sufficiency. They brought their own supplies, hunted for their own food, and found their own shelter in the wilderness. The mountain men would gather at a yearly rendezvous to resupply, to trade their pelts, to drink whisky, to face off in contests of skill and strength, and to fight and gamble in a carnival before departing again for solitary lives in the mountains. After the last great rendezvous of 1838, the silk hat, not the beaver hat, became the item of London fashion. Fur prices plunged and their days of glory were over. But mountain men like Jedediah Smith and Jim Bridger, who had explored the West, turned into figures of the frontier romance. Storytellers mythologized their lives, placing them in the narrative form of the heroic epic.

I was introduced to Alaska mountain men by Joe Mattie, the owner of the Alaska Raw Fur Company, who flew his small plane out to these trappers' cabins to buy the highest quality Alaska furs. To understand the trapping life, I interviewed key informants like Mattie, and I also met trappers by buying beaver hats and fur mittens from them. This led to a correspondence with isolated trappers, by letter at infrequent intervals, whenever they got to town and opened their post office boxes. In the summer, when they came to town to resupply, I would pick up the beaver hats and mittens, learn how to comb the fur, and interview them about their lives. A cherished genre of stories, for example, was the mail-order bride, in which they advertised in trapping magazines for a woman to join them in the wilderness. I also went to trapping school, where experienced trappers taught novices how to set up traps and snares, explained fish and game regulations, and described the habits and habitats of beaver, wolves, and wolverine. I met legendary trappers who resembled nineteenth-century mountain men, embracing the heavy labor of cutting new trails, their trails becoming roads for those who followed.

Randy Brown

What drove Randy Brown's passion into going beyond was *The Big Sky* by A. B. Guthrie. The story centers on Boone Caudill, who travels to the Rockies, living as a trapper and explorer, becoming an untamed mountain man. In the summer of 1976, Randy Brown went about as deep into the wilderness as it is possible to go. With a friend, Little John, he stowed a few supplies into two canoes and pushed off into the Yukon River. They took a twenty-five-pound sack of rice, a twenty-five-pound sack of beans, and a five-gallon bucket of tallow. That was about it for store grub; they planned to be gone for a year.

They floated eighty miles down the Yukon, then pulled their canoes another sixty miles up a tributary river. Lining the loaded canoes and hiking up the river was slow, heavy, wet work. They built log cabins with hand tools and cut out trapline trails. With all this work, their food went pretty fast; they were down to a few beans when they shot a moose. Eventually they learned where to find and how to hunt the caribou, rendering out every ounce of fat. Warm, tough clothing was the next absolute necessity, and it, too, had to come from the wilderness. Using a sewing awl and caribou hides with the hair left on, they sewed pants and parkas with hoods trimmed with wolf ruffs. Their sweat softened the skins. Before long, they were dressed completely in skin clothing, and living from kill to kill.

The "Hoffman" Family

Living out the mountain man romance and carrying forward into time the American pioneer tradition was Robert Hoffman's life dream. In 1958 he saw an advertisement for a trapping line in the magazine *Fur-Fish-Game*, but he ended up in the army and then on a farm in upstate New York. Thirty years later, after his divorce, he saw an advertisement for the same trapline he had wanted to buy in 1958. When a trapper buys a trapline in Alaska, he is not buying the land but rather the traps and shelters on the trapline and the right to trap in this region by an informal gentleman's agreement among the trappers. The owner of the trapline said he got all kinds of responses to his advertisement, but Robert Hoffman was the only man who enclosed a check for $500 and that made it a deal. Suffering from ill health and financial reversals in upstate New York, Robert Hoffman lay sick in the back seat of the truck while his two boys drove to Alaska. When they flew into the wilderness, they found a fourteen-by-sixteen-foot cabin along the Kantishna River and a few traplines. Over several years they turned the cabin and trapline into a wilderness estate, with a log house that looks like it's straight out of the nineteenth century and gardens watered with an ingenious system of hoses that draw from the river.

The Hoffman family gets by on about $12,000 a year. Fur prices fluctuate and rarely supply even these modest cash needs. There are far easier ways to make a living than trapping in the sparse interior forest of Alaska. Their lives are a grueling daily round of rising early in the morning, starting a fire in the cold, cooking breakfast for their sled dogs, harnessing them up to check their traplines, and taking shelter at night in cabins along the trapline, where they skin their furs and repair their equipment. They owe nobody money. They get about sixty percent of their cash income from furs, and they make crafts for sale to tourists—like a handcrafted salmon wheel, a perfect miniature of the salmon wheel Robert Hoffman uses—and they guide tourists and build log cabins in the summer.

Killing of animals is never easy, the Hoffmans emphasize; they have to steel themselves to the task each time. They say, "It's our duty when you catch an animal to get out there as quick as you can." But living free for as long as you can is the right way to live, they believe—surely a better life for an animal than being raised as a commodity on a factory farm. "Animals rarely if ever die of old age," they point out. "If you have ever seen an animal eaten alive by a pack of wolves, you realize that a well-placed bullet is an easier death."

Freedom is the driving theme in the Hoffmans' narrative of their lives. They see their lives as bearing witness to America's essences. They define freedom as not living according to other people's expectations and not devoting their lives to the pursuit of success, fame, and glory. They can slow down and savor things, see the trees and the rivers, and glimpse the "active presence of God." In the wilderness, they feel a spiritual exaltation. In some mystical moments, the boundary between self, earth, and sky disappears and they feel at one with the natural world. This communion with nature is something the trappers don't often discuss with each other or outsiders. The Hoffmans use the language of religion. "From the wilderness, we learn who God is. You feel a oneness. God becomes real in a way he hadn't before. He is with us all the time. People have isolated themselves from the natural world and the declarations it makes so loudly of the active presence of God. People try to fulfill themselves with fame and glory, with wealth and possessions, all avenues of 'success.' Yet in the end they cry out like Solomon, 'This too is meaningless, a striving after the wind.'" I asked one of the Hoffman sons how he could stand to live alone, for seven months at a time, by himself in a shelter on one of their traplines. But he doesn't live alone. He is with God, I came to realize. When I asked him, he said, simply, "Yes, that is right."

When the other Hoffman son goes to Germany, invited by a man he guided in the wilderness, freedom is what the audience wants to hear about. The Germans are fascinated by the life of a trapper in Alaska. They are fascinated by the idea that you can still live in the modern world and be self-sufficient.

The Hoffmans see themselves as genuine mountain men, as "real trappers." They distance themselves from the playacting of the impostors who pretend to be mountain men—the silly weekenders who drive their trucks to faux fur rendezvous where they buy mountain men paraphernalia, talk with a twang, and hide their coolers of beer under Indian blankets. The Hoffmans identify themselves as "free trappers" to distinguish themselves not only from these faux mountain men but also from those nineteenth-century trappers who were not independent but who were virtually indentured to the fur company that supplied them.

Richard Gardner

An Alaska mountain man and trapper, Richard Gardner knows cold, not the "I'm chilly and need a sweater" type of cold but the icy bite that gnaws into your bones and paralyzes your muscles, a numbing, violent cold that sucks your breath from you and makes you shiver so violently that you want to scream at the top of your lungs for a reprieve but can't inhale the breath to do so.[1]

One of the biggest dangers to trappers is getting caught in the overflow of the rivers they are crossing on their snowmachines or dogsleds. Groundwater, melted ice, seeps between the frozen lake or slough ice and the covering layer of snow. Areas of overflow can thin the ice to the thinness of a dinner plate. Breaking through the ice when the outside air temperature is forty below is a sucker punch from nature that leaves you dazed and violently gasping. The water—insulated from freezing under thick snow cover—freezes instantly when exposed to the frigid air of forty degrees below zero.

Caught in overflow, you suffer muscle spasms, involuntary drop kicks that attempt to loosen your diaphragm cramped into inaction at the sudden immersion. Limbs numb instantly. Your shocked heart

Mountain man Richard Gardner prepares to go hunting. Courtesy Chris Batin.

struggles to keep blood flowing to your extremities. People die from sudden immersion in cold water. The only thing worse is crawling out. Ice forms immediately, overloading the skin's cold receptors, creating what doctors call the "cold shock response." Such cold is the boreal equivalent of the grim reaper, always waiting for a moment's carelessness, an oversight, or just plain bad luck.

Self-control and competence in the wilderness are essential for survival. You must breathe slowly. Breathe too hard and you freeze your lungs. Remove your gloves, and a minute later, your fingers turn into broomsticks. Wear the wrong clothes or drop through a stretch of river, and the chances are you will succumb to the same fate as the character in Jack London's tale "To Build a Fire." Richard Gardner hugs his kids and kisses his wife goodbye. Thinking about such possible mistakes keeps him wary and watchful.

Trappers delight in telling great survival tales in the wilderness, like the story of Hugh Glass, wounded and mauled by a bear, and coming out "shining," mountain man talk for walking in glory. In 1822, Glass responded to an advertisement in the *Missouri Gazette and Public Adviser* to join a group of a hundred men ascending the Missouri River to become part of a fur trapping and trading venture. While scouting for camp meat, Glass surprised a grizzly who had two cubs with her. The grizzly attacked, and Glass wrestled her to the ground, killing the bear with his knife, but only after being mauled with portions of his back stripped off; he was unable to walk. His companions, hearing his screams, found him with the bear on top of him. Jim Bridger and John Fitzgerald volunteered to stay with Glass until he died. But the pair of men left him for dead, fleeing an Indian attack, taking Glass' rifle, knife, and gear. Glass regained consciousness and despite a broken leg, lacerations that exposed broken ribs, and festering wounds, he set his own leg and crawled or limped the two hundred miles to the nearest fort. He subsisted on roots and berries and drove away two wolves from a kill so he could eat the raw meat. He allowed maggots to eat at the dead flesh on his back to prevent gangrene, and eventually he reached Fort Kiowa.

Richard Gardner pulls on his beaver parka and Carhartts, carrying traps, snares, and a chainsaw, and heads off to his traplines. During the winter, Gardner and his brother John run three separate traplines. The

Richard Gardner in front of his trapping cabin. Courtesy Chris Batin.

longest and most treacherous runs through the Tanana River, sixty miles through remote river and slough country, a harsh, forsaken land that takes five days to cover by snowmobile. The other two can be checked in two or three days. He is an uncommon man, a square peg that doesn't fit society's well-rounded mold for success. This forty-three-year-old never attended college, but he knows electrical engineering. He owns several remote homesteads he cleared, with cabins he built himself. He flies a 1947 PA-11 that he must hand-crank the propeller to start.

Gardner is a jack-of-all-trades. He sells pelts, but his trapping brings in only about $5,000 a season. A few Alaska trappers make more from their pelts, as much as $15,000 annually when fur prices are high. To generate more money from his traplines, Gardner has embraced the handicraft trade, in which he tans the hides and makes mittens and fur hats at far greater profit than just raw fur sales. To get the cash he needs for trapping and to support his family, he earns income from building cabinets and log cabins and works as a big-game guide and as a warehouse manager during the summer fire season. With only so many hours in a day and government regulations that dictate regular checking of traps, there is a limit to how much money a trapper can make. These are the economics of trapping. There are easier ways to make a living.

Chris Batin

Richard Gardner apprenticed himself to Chris Batin when he came to Alaska from southwest Ohio. Chris gave him a few tests and trials to see if he was going to make the grade or if he was nothing but another wilderness wannabe. Chris made a living off the Alaska mountains, trapping, hunting and fishing, and pioneering for a living. He loaned him traps and found Gardner had the drive and heart of a mountain man and a code of honor.

"We are majestic bull moose, not following the herd but making our own way," Chris explains. "We respect all those who love the mountains in their own ways, but we have our own definition and love affair with the mountain. There are those who embrace the challenge of climbing Mount Everest or any other noteworthy mountain with its waiting groups, herd-mentality camps, and lines of people all climbing in the same manner. We blaze our own trails away from the crowds, choosing our own Everest to conquer, whether it's being the best trapper in the area or claiming with simple satisfaction what few athletes in the world can claim: We survive winters in the Alaska wilderness. After a barrage of traffic noise and the incessant idle talk that goes nowhere, the trapper wants to—no needs to—retreat to the wilderness and a return to sanity.

"Any trapper worth his salt finds beauty in the quarry he pursues. Trappers are romantics; for a man to kill a thing of beauty causes pain. He is not just taking the animal's life and pelt. He knows that he is removing forever this beautiful animal. For most this realization hurts. Some acclimatize. But few trappers take from an animal its fur and fail to notice the luster. For a large proportion there is often a pause, for some a microsecond, for others long minutes, to be thankful, to see and appreciate this animal that the trapper may be the first to hold and behold. Animals of the cold north live in the same temperatures as the

Mountain man Chris Batin hiking. Courtesy Chris Batin.

trappers, subject to the same disasters of injury, dehydration, cold, and starvation. We ask the lynx or marten to absolve us and to understand the circle of life and that their skin and their lives are appreciated. It is an act that honors the animals, as it does the trapper who embraces such a tradition. We know the absolutes that await us all."

Trappers are so tied to the land that they want to be buried in or have their ashes spread over the portion of the land they love most. Thomas McElroy was one of them, a giant of a man who lived in the Talkeetna Mountains from the 1960s to the early 1990s. He lived most of his life as a mountain man and rarely traveled into town. Life was full circle for him. After he died he wanted to become a perpetual part of the streams and plants that nourished him and the animals. He reasoned his remains would give life to future generations of the moose and furbearers he pursued, and the plants and trees that had sheltered him. Up the trailless wilderness of the Talkeetna Mountains near Stephan Lake you can find a headstone that is a testimonial to all who follow in his footsteps: "This Man Lived Life." Fellow mountain man Jim Bailey, who has a cabin down the lake from where McElroy lived, is the person who spread Tom's ashes and placed his gravestone near Stephan Lake. Because Bailey and Chris Batin shared the ways of the wilderness and had the brushes with death that are stock-in-trade for mountain men, he instructed Chris to spread his ashes in the Talkeetna Mountains. This obligation is an honor that will draw Chris from anywhere on earth to complete.

"Modern-day Alaska mountain men reenact the primordial heroic tale—answering the call of the unknown, facing tests and trials, feeling the ecstacy of fighting against adversity and being the one left standing," says Chris. "You stand in the face of the storm and dare it to take you, shouting that you will not be defeated. Battered and bruised, you stand, empowered. High government officials, college professors, and heads of corporations pay thousands of dollars to be guided into the wilderness to sample for only a week what a mountain man lives for a lifetime. They challenge themselves to see if they have what it takes to make the physical and spiritual journey, to survive the elemental tests along the way, the personal triumphs and challenges that make men stand tall."

For men like Chris Batin, stories have turned into lives. When I asked Alaska trappers why they had chosen to live such tough lives, they often brought up, without any suggestion, the influence of stories—Jack London's *Call of the Wild*, Farley Mowat's *Lost in the Barrens*, and the Davy Crockett and Daniel Boone television shows of their childhoods. Daniel Boone was a power figure, and Chris admired him for his exploration of the Kentucky wilderness. Chris and his younger brother imitated his actions, practicing how to throw an ax. In one episode, Boone cut himself with an ax and had his daughter put bear fat on the wound. Chris tried to put beef fat on his own cuts to see if it would heal them. He and his brother relished being chased by "Indians," venturing into areas that were off-limits like the Wright-Patterson Air Force Base in Dayton, Ohio. When patrol cars tried to corner them, they would disappear into the woods.

In his childhood, Chris Batin and his brother in their imaginations became mountain men. They rode their bikes through rundown neighborhoods where dogs ran after them. But these were not dogs, they were wild wolves; the boys were not riding their bikes but riding their horses, attempting to escape the wolves to save their very lives. They would stop off at the General Store on Springfield Street to "resupply" for the day. They trapped and snared rabbits and muskrats, shot groundhogs, and speared carp in the rivers. Too poor to buy waders, they waded in shorts and tennis shoes, impervious to cold and pain because they were mountain men. They would build campfires to prove their fire-building skills and cook bacon stolen from the refrigerator, the closest food they could find to the "hump fat" that the mountain men ate.

In middle age, Chris can still recall the words to the theme song:

Daniel Boone was a man,
Yes, a big man!
He was brave, he was fearless
And as tough as a mighty oak tree.

He read Farley Mowat's *Lost in the Barrens*, the story of two boys who were stranded in the wilderness and who had to use their wits and skills to survive. He gravitated toward similar books, like Jean Craighead George's *My Side of the Mountain*, a story about a young boy who survives in the woods on his own. He absorbed every word, emulating the boy's actions, building snares and deadfalls. When he shot his first rabbit and dressed it as he had read in storybooks, his mother cooked it for the family. He was a woodsman.

The film *Jeremiah Johnson* mesmerized him. Chris left the theater stunned, playing the scenes over and over again in his mind, struggling to remember each detail. When the film appeared on television, he recorded it, watching it countless times, memorizing the lines.

He says, "Jeremiah Johnson was the hero we needed. He experienced difficulties as we did and he overcame them. He started out with nothing but eventually acquired a .50-caliber Hawken, the best wilderness rifle a mountain man could have. Jeremiah Johnson was his own man, a free man, and answered to no one. In the mountains, Jeremiah Johnson becomes the master of his own life, acquires skills and power, and he achieves honor. Johnson learns that the power he sought in the mountain has been within himself all along."

Chris Batin has achieved more than he would have if he had not left his family and gone to live in Alaska. The Alaska wilderness gave him unusual experience and competence and opened up career possibilities he would never otherwise have had. He became an outdoors writer. As of 2006, he had eighty-nine regional writing and photography awards to his credit. He is currently on the mastheads as a contributing editor for *Travel Age West, Western Outdoors, Alaska Coast,* and *Outdoor Life* magazines. Chris turned life in the wilderness into art, through romantic outdoors writing and photography. In his outdoors writing, the struggle to survive in the wilderness is transformed into a metaphor for the struggle to survive adversity in other realms. The triumph lies in overcoming the shortcoming of the self, physical or mental. The triumph lies in facing whatever must be faced and standing tall. Stay calm; think the situation through; find a way, even if this road was not on your original life map. These are his guidelines for survival not only in the Alaska wilderness but in all situations of adversity.

Trappers like the Hoffmans, Richard Gardner, and Chris Batin attempt to live out the romance of the mountain man. The reality is not nearly so exotic. After all, Chris Batin is a writer and photographer who travels the world. Richard Gardner lives with his wife in a small Alaska town and he merely makes forays into the wilderness. The Hoffmans as well are not far from the city of Fairbanks. These men have used the narrative of the mountain man to give meaning to their lives, to give their lives heroic proportions. Others seize the identity of the mountain man but, as I show in chapter 4, turn its narrative into a mask for psychopathology.

CHAPTER 2

....

The Pioneer Women

The helicopter set down my husband, a petroleum geologist, on an empty beach in the Alaska wilderness. Far in the distance he spied two tiny figures walking toward him. The figures turned into two young women, one with a three-month-old baby on her back, the other with a 12-gauge shotgun on her back. These young women turned out to be married to men mining the beaches for gold. They were living there by choice. No hot water, no running water, no electricity, no Nordstrom's. No medical care. A newborn baby yet! Who are these people?

—Kay Mero, California Historical Trust

The image of the pioneer woman with a baby on her back and a shotgun on her shoulder has become an icon of the American frontier romance. In this chapter, I describe the wilderness women who used this narrative to construct their identities, to define who they are for themselves and for others. Their life stories create a heroic identity of an independent, tough woman, challenged by a barely acknowledged reality, the embarrassing problem that they have actually followed a man into the wilderness.

Jill Hannon, for example, appropriated the symbol of the pioneer women for her own narrative of identity when she posed for a photograph, taken by her husband, Dennis, in the spring of 1984 at Deadfish Lake.[1] In the photograph Jill mugs for the camera, standing tall, one foot firmly on a bear carcass, one arm cradling her baby, her other arm proudly holding an upright rifle. She is playacting, but her play is ironic. Jill Hannon and her husband are living deep in the wilderness, in a cabin they built themselves, only a dugout with a stovepipe sticking out. Jill actually shot this bear on whose carcass she is standing, when it threatened her family. She is communicating her identification with the pioneer mother of covered wagon days while distancing herself from the image through an over-the-top, mocking pose.

So is her friend Laurel Tyrrell, who also posed with her baby and shotgun in another enactment of this iconic scene in the early years of her life in the wilderness. Appropriating childhood stories, she calls this period her "Daniel Boone days." She titles her life story "Living Out the Frontier Myth in the Twenty-First Century."[2] She constructs her identity as a pioneer woman, who has created a community on the American frontier.

The Public Narrative of the Pioneer Women

Laurel Tyrrell burst into my office at the University of Alaska like a cannonball, wearing blue jeans and a faded pink sweatshirt, towing her six-year-old son, a cheerful little boy with hair the color of carrots. She had a bone to pick with me. She took exception to an article I had written on wilderness women featuring a cabin-dweller named Marilyn Jesmain. Leaving her luxury home in the Midwest and starting a new life in her sixties, Marilyn lived in a cabin with no running water and an outhouse. When the temperature dropped to forty degrees below zero and Marilyn did not want to make the trek to the outhouse, she used a Lady J, a plastic device in the shape of a J that lets a lady relieve herself discreetly standing up when plumbing isn't available.

Marilyn Jesmain was not an authentic pioneer woman, Laurel insisted. She was nothing but a poseur. Sure, she lived in a cabin, but she could run out any time for an espresso at the coffee shop or a shower at the laundromat. Laurel and her friends claimed the title of true pioneer women. They lived in Central, over a dangerous mountain pass where they and their families built their own cabins, homesteaded, hunted moose and caribou for their food, and shot bears. When I asked to be introduced to these "true" pioneer women, Laurel invited me to tea, telling me to be there by April, before some of the women left to go deeper into the wilderness. As she marched out of my office, she fired a parting shot. That impostor Marilyn Jesmain had said she liked to sit in the nude in the woods outside her cabin. Did she now? Well, she sure was going to need plenty of mosquito repellent in intimate places.

Driving to Central to meet the pioneer women was a tough journey, even in my four-wheel-drive Jeep. On Eagle Summit, fierce winds and blowing snow could create frightening whiteouts where you feel you are bouncing inside a ping-pong ball. In a whiteout, you cannot see the hood of your car, you cannot tell the road from the sky. People in more than one vehicle had plunged to their death off Eagle Summit. On ridges in the mountains lie gold mines, some remains from the turn-of-the-century mining days while others are active mines. Gold had been discovered in the Circle Mining District in 1893 on Birch Creek, and prospectors fanned out to nearby streams, Bonanza Creek, Mastodon Creek, Independence Creek, the color of their gold recognizable to an expert eye. The town of Central had been the center of the mining district, a supply and distribution center for the miners in the early twentieth century. Now the population had dwindled to about 120 people, some of whom still mined for gold.

The Tyrrells' two-story log cabin was festooned with moose antlers. This was the second log house that Laurel and her husband, Rick, had built, cutting and peeling the logs themselves. They had outgrown their first twelve-by-sixteen-foot cabin after their three sons were born. Now they use their first cabin as a storage shed. We parked our Jeep next to several trucks, many with the keys still in the ignition. In her master's thesis at the University of Alaska in 2002, "Living Out the Frontier Myth in the Twenty-First Century," Laurel Tyrrell portrays her life as a pioneer woman, calling such neighborly trust part of the "Code of the North," appropriating imagery from Jack London and Robert Service. The code of the North she defined as "a system of hospitality involving helpfulness, treatment of others, and obligations of giving and sharing.[3] In a community with few paying jobs, people operated within an informal system of reciprocity in which physical labor, clothing, meat, or cranberries might be exchanged for a haircut, fixing an outboard engine, or supplying power to someone's freezer." The code of the North was a system of social norms far more thoughtful, personal, and extended over time than a system of simple economic barter. Brad Snow helped a man in Central, for example, with the tedious task of mending his fishnet. When Snow's wife was about to deliver her baby, the man flew his plane out to fish camp to bring back a close female friend of Snow's wife to keep her company and help her out.

Central is not an incorporated town and has no local law enforcement. Central has its own homegrown ways of dealing with outlaws, reminiscent of western stories and validating residents' images of themselves. Locals labeled a feud between two Central families ending in a gunfight in a bar as "The Shoot-out at the O.K. Corral," appropriating imagery from the 1881 shoot-out in Tombstone, Arizona, pitting Wyatt Earp and Doc Holliday against the Clanton gang. In the Central shoot-out, one furious woman got her semiautomatic rifle from her truck and shot bullets into the front of the Central Motor Inn. A man from the other family pulled out his gun, ducking and firing, over and over again. The people in the bar crawled under pool tables or ran for cover in the basement. When the fight was over, one man lay dead, shot through his chest, another man had a gunshot wound in his shoulder, and a woman had taken shots in her abdomen.

As in western films, people who cause trouble are run out of town. Both families were ostracized until they pulled out of Central. All sharing ceased, no one would sell them gas, no business would serve them a meal. If they appeared in public, silence would fall. The people of Central told such stories of how miscreants had been treated in the past as a method of social control, to warn wrongdoers about what awaited them. The stories also romanticized life in this remote community by associating events in the present with the West of the imagination.

Ten pioneer women sat in the living room, dressed in their Central best, blue jeans and sweatshirts without holes. On a side table a tea was laid out, with such delicacies as sausage made from ground bear, moose, and caribou. Laurel had brought out her heirloom silver, which gleamed next to the paper plates. Her cabin had no running water so she used paper whenever she could. Her cabin also had no refrigerator. In the spot in the kitchen where a refrigerator usually stands was a trapdoor leading to an old-fashioned root cellar. The permafrost kept the food cold.

My husband was so startled at the sight of the ten pioneer women sprawled in the cabin that he nearly knocked over the two guns standing by the kitchen door. I doubted the guns were loaded. "Of course, they were loaded," he retorted. "Why else would you have a gun by the door? You might as well have a broomstick!" The guns were loaded, Laurel later confirmed. When a bear barreled into your yard, you needed to be able to fire a warning shot fast. If the bear broke in, you needed to be able to fire a killing shot.

Laurel had been forced to fire a killing shot when she was hunting caribou for the family's winter meat supply. She was at the family's summer subsistence camp with her two young sons and her father-in-law. "Grandpa hadn't put on his hearing aid, and the bear was ripping the tarp above his tent." During my visit, Laurel begins, "My five-year-old was in that tent. I jumped out of my tent in my skivvies. The bear ignored my warning shot. I waited until he was down on all fours to shoot him because I didn't want to shoot when he was standing right next to Grandpa." The grizzly weighed over 350 pounds, and Laurel had to skin the bear, drag the innards to the river, and wash the campsite so the blood and odor wouldn't attract other bears. She and her young boys shoveled out the blood-soaked stones, skinned the bear, dragged the guts and carcass to the Colleen River, and stretched out the hide. "Killing the Bear" is one of Laurel's cherished stories, communicating the identity she has created: a woman who is tough and competent; who can kill a bear, skin it, and clean up the camp; who can protect (without her husband) her young sons and aging father-in-law on a sandbar in the wilderness.

I turned on my tape recorder, and the pioneer women launched into other cherished stories. These stories about their lives in the wilderness were oft-told tales for public consumption. They were the official life stories told to strangers, what Jacqueline Wiersma calls in life history research the "press release."[4] The storytelling reminded me of a quilting bee, each of the women adding her own brightly designed square of material to the community narrative. The narrative tone of these public stories was upbeat and humorous, quite different from the tone of the private life stories I would hear later.

"Why did you choose this lifestyle?" I asked the women. Several women bristled at the word *lifestyle*. The label was frivolous. They had not chosen a lifestyle, they told me, but a "life way." No rat race. No rush. No nine-to-five life. They followed the time clock of nature. They had time to be mindful, to see the birds and the foxes, to smell the wildflowers and catalog them, to walk with their dogs in the wilderness and see the beauty of the natural world. They could spend their time in artistic creation—sewing fur, writing stories of the pioneer life, beading, and making sculptured birchbark flowers. They could change the rhythm of their lives with the change in the seasons, working hard in summer and slowing down in winter. They could live in and savor the moment rather than rushing through the short time they had been given on the earth.

Coming to Alaska was a life transition and a philosophical decision about what counted. They rejected the artificial. "In the city you have to put up a front," said "Cindy." "You have to put on makeup. We have clearer focus on priorities." Her father-in-law kept harping on her to wear makeup. "Well, Dad, we ought to consider ourselves lucky," said her husband. "At least she shaves her legs and her armpits, which a lot of the women up there don't do."

Their narratives displayed their pride in their self-sufficiency and competence. "My parents ask us why we live this way," one of the women said. "But watch the news. You just guffaw. Remember the news story where they interviewed people about the storm that crippled the city? The power went off, and this woman was so astonished when she found she could make coffee on her charcoal grill."

This story was topped with another narrative displaying the ingenuity the women had to have to live at the edge of the earth. Catalog stores wouldn't send packages to post office box numbers. So they invented addresses. "I said we live on 1 Taildragger Lane," said Susan. The audience laughed. "We have a plane (a taildragger) and airstrip," she explained. "The voice at the end of the line asked if this address was current. I said, 'Yip.'"

The women took pride in making deliberate decisions about what was important in life. "I have made a choice to do this. I know a lot of people who couldn't do it. When people ask us why we live here, I say, spend a week with us. Once you've felt the peace, you will understand. You are so relaxed. Everyone is happier," said one woman, the others nodding their agreement.

They enjoyed impressing their families and strangers with pioneer images that linked their lives with America's past. One woman related: "I told my mom we got a new washer. She asked what kind I bought. 'A wringer washer,' I told her. My mom just said, 'Oh, my God.' This one lady who drove by was so fascinated that I was doing my laundry in the wringer that she got out her camera."

The women's narratives were part of a tradition of storytelling in Central, its purpose the social construction of a pioneer community. Old-timers told stories of life in the wilderness both to showcase their own toughness and ingenuity and to communicate the social norms of life in a pioneer town. One story went: "Johnny Lake told my kids dishes were never a problem with him. He would eat on the clean dishes, then turn them over, and he had another set of dishes. After that, he'd put some water in a big tub and let them soak for several weeks, then wash them up and be ready again."[5] Other stories were tales of moose gorings, of months recovering alone in a cabin.

The quilt of stories the women were stitching together for public display portrayed Central as a pioneer version of Brigadoon, rising from the mist, keeping alive bedrock American virtues under siege in the modern world. The women cast themselves as the heroes, but their narrative also featured a villain—the National Park Service. In their telling, the agency sought to destroy the life of an authentic frontier community in an effort to create a fraudulent image of untouched wilderness. Their life way was under siege. The small gold miners had been driven out of the region, unable to comply with federal regulations limiting sediment discharge. The Central region, commercial gold mining country for the past hundred years, had been turned into the wilderness of the environmentalists' imagination, now legalized with such designations as the "Yukon Flats National Wildlife Refuge" and the "Birch Creek Wild and Scenic River." In this contest between the women's pioneer narrative of the Central region and the National Park Service's wilderness narrative, designed to preserve the natural world, the wilderness narrative had triumphed. This has practical effects on their ability to live out the American pioneering story. The Tyrrells' trapping cabin, for example, sits on public land. If the Tyrrells renew the permit at five-year intervals, complying with complicated regulations without error, they can continue to use their cabin and their sons can use it but not their grandchildren. As the joke in the region goes, soon the Park Service will hire college students and put the students in pioneer costumes, portraying the authentic frontier people of Central who have been forced out.

The Private Narratives of the Pioneer Women

"You are not getting the whole story," Pam Haskin whispered to me, in a private moment after I had turned off the tape recorder at the gathering Laurel had set up to tell the stories of the wilderness women. I arranged to meet Pam alone in her cabin the next morning to get the rest of the story.

"Don't believe the jokes you heard. This is a rough life," Pam told me. She started to cry. "My family thought I was crazy to come here. They were angry at me for moving so far away. Dutiful daughters stay near their families."

I asked Laurel Tyrrell and Pam Haskin to collaborate in later research and uncover the personal stories within the public romance the women wove.[6] Narrative psychology emphasizes the role of the audience in the telling of life stories. To whom is the story told and for what purposes? Different audiences elicit different life stories. The story of life in Central that I had heard at the tea was the story for public consumption, portraying tough and inventive pioneer women of the frontier. The private stories the women told later did not contradict the public story. But the private stories took on somber coloring and dealt with more personal, sometimes tragic, themes, such as a history of drug use. These personal stories can be placed into three thematic categories: (1) the redemption story, (2) the quest for the dream man, and (3) two in the wilderness. Some women told life histories with varying combinations of these three themes.

THE REDEMPTION STORY

This version of the frontier romance is a variation of the master narrative that McAdams labels "the redemptive self."[7] Personal suffering and tragedy is transformed into acts of goodness. The Central women who told this version of the frontier romance narrated it as a story of rebirth. The journey to Alaska, which could begin as a casual adventure, became a turning point and the decision to stay in Alaska became a life transition.

When asked what the story of her life should say, "Jane" gave it the title "Bad Girl Gone Good." Abused as a young girl after the death of her mother, she escaped into fantasy. Jane dreamed she was living back in America's pioneer days. She should have been born in another age when she could go west in a covered wagon. As a young woman she became a drug addict, a college dropout, and an unwed mother. When she came to Alaska on a visit she found a "white world of snow and ice" where no one knew who she had been, where she could compose a new life. She sold everything she had and returned with nothing of her former life that she could not carry in a backpack and a duffel bag. When Jane volunteered to serve on the emergency medical team in Central, her history as a drug addict did not cause people to look askance and bar her from the position of medic. She became the squad leader of the emergency medical team. When a small boy riding a three-wheeler hit a tree, Jane and her team treated him on top of the pool table at the local bar. The medical helicopter hadn't arrived, and the child started to lose consciousness. Jane knew that small children stay strong and you don't think there's too much wrong with them, but when they die, they die quickly. Jane and her team pulled the little boy through.

Many serious accidents happen in an unsettled region where people construct their own houses, mine for gold, fly small planes, shoot game for meat, and travel by snowmobile through the forest and creeks in temperatures reaching fifty degrees below zero. Standard training for emergency medical technicians is based on urban assumptions, such as the assumption that the accident will happen near a road. In Central, accidents often happened on a trail far from any road. Jane had to learn to improvise, for example, making a stretcher from branches on the trail to bring back a snowmobiler who had hit a tree deep in the wilderness. Jane received the honor of the region's "Emergency Medical Technician of the Year."

The frontier romance brought Jane to Alaska. But the narrative was more than myth. The realities of life in a remote wilderness community, a place where people with a past were commonplace, where people were needed regardless of past mistakes, enabled Jane to land a role crucial to the community, expand her talents, make life-giving contributions to a new society, and find redemption.

THE QUEST FOR THE DREAM MAN

The public, official narrative of the pioneer women took the form of a quest narrative, the search for a frontier life more meaningful than the rat race. Their private narratives emphasized more personal quests, most commonly the quest for the man of their dreams. A particularly romantic example was the story of the mail-order bride, a staple story line of romance novels: The heroine possesses the courage to travel to a new and unknown world and marry a stranger. She must also possess the magical power of making him fall in love with her. Since the woman in this romance is starting all over again, sometimes from a difficult past, the mail-order bride story can be viewed as a variant of the redemption narrative.

"Laurie" was a biker who wanted to shed the rough biking life that had left her with nothing but bleeding ulcers. She came across a magazine advertisement in *Ruralite*—a miner was searching for a woman to come to Alaska. Laurie sold her Harley and bought a one-way ticket to Alaska. She had just enough money left to get back home. The man waiting for her at the airport turned out to be muscled with thick black hair and an easy grin. In his personal story line, he cast himself as a cowboy, tough and self-sufficient, a man who, had he lived in the old west, would have reached for his gun in a confrontation with the villainous federal officials trying to appropriate his property. He brought Laurie to a log house he had built himself with windows on every side that looked out at the mountains. But even a guy who resembled Rhett Butler faced competition from other men in the region who were also looking for a woman. In the North, Laurie had many marital opportunities, which she didn't have in her previous life. But she stuck with him. She learned the craft of beading when she tried to bead moccasins for him. Beading became her business, and she invented original arctic designs. She put up a website for other beaders, wrote two books on beading that sold well, and held wilderness retreats for beaders in her

Alaska cabin. On the frontier, she was no longer a biker but had become a respected businesswoman.

Finding a dream mate in the wilderness was a common quest story of pioneer women and had many romantic variations. Disillusioned with the America of the sixties, Judy Ferguson calls herself a hippie chick "carrying out the legacy of the old pioneers."[8] She wanted three things out of life: a cabin open to the wind, a horse, and a good man. Hitchhiking with her girlfriend to Big Delta, she met a woodsman, the type of true trapper whom other trappers regarded as the genuine article. She and her girlfriend had left the road, walked into the forest, and found a log cabin with a tree growing on top of the cabin's sod roof. Nearby stood a sorrel horse tethered to a spruce tree. "There's your horse. And there's your cabin," said her girlfriend. "Now let's go inside and see what your man is like." After raising three children with her husband, Reb, on a homesite accessible only by dogsled or boat, Judy found a new passion. Her life in the wilderness had given her a store of original material for a career as

Judy Ferguson bathed her baby in a pot on the stove. Living in cabins without running water, wilderness women come up with inventive methods for bathing, brushing their teeth, and washing their hair. Courtesy Judy Ferguson.

a freelance writer. She wrote an autobiography of her life in the Alaska wilderness, how she found her own "Blue Hills," her personal promised land, and she wrote other stories of the region, such as a history of the quirky pioneers who had come from Yugoslavia and settled the Delta region almost a century before.

Among the pioneer women, the personal quest story typically centered on the search for a soul mate and on the rigors of raising children in the wilderness. This version of the frontier romance followed the classic story line of the heroic life pattern: (1) the call to adventure, (2) the road of tests and trials, and (3) the winning of the trophy, the life-renewing boon. But this life narrative presented the pioneer women with an interpretive problem that the next version of this story explores. After the Women's Movement, their audience could view their life story not as a heroic narrative but as a narrative of subordination, a life without honor.

TWO IN THE WILDERNESS: IN THE SHELTER OF EACH OTHER

The narrative of two in the wilderness is a metaphor for one of the most satisfying of human experiences: a husband and wife setting out on the journey of life together, facing their new world with all its dangers and difficulties, in the shelter of each other. In Central, some pioneer women lived out this story in the most extreme and literal sense. They lived with their husbands in isolated trapping cabins in the Alaska wilderness where they faced the dangers of extreme cold and marauding bears. They were proud of their courage and skills. Nonetheless, to follow your man was not a respected theme in the life stories of modern, autonomous women. They downplayed this theme, especially in the public narratives they told. "I came for the love of a man," as Laurel Tyrrell finally admitted. "Why should this be without honor?"

In the frontier romance of Central, no couple embodied the two in the wilderness tale more than "Jack and Jill." Looking out at the blue and silver mountains from her residence hall at the University of Alaska Fairbanks, Jill told herself, "This is it!" She decided to attend the meetings of the Alaska Trappers Association and look over the possibilities.

She chose "Jack," who had lived for many years on a homestead in the Goldstream Valley in Fairbanks.

On a canoe trip on the Yukon River, Jack and Jill found a spot to build a log cabin that looked like a picture from their childhood storybooks. They dropped four thousand pounds of gear at the Indian village of Circle and started packing their worldly goods into the wilderness, stopping to build shelters every ten miles or so because that was as far as they thought they could walk if they needed to get out. Jill loved training her dog team and hiking the hills with Jack, taking the dogs with them. "I've always been one to think, whatever we do we do together," she said.

"Shooting the Bear" was one of Jill's emblematic stories, like Laurel's bear story, but given a different interpretation. One morning Jack was doing his "morning business with his pants down." He heard a rustling behind him, turned to look, and spooked a juvenile black bear. Jack started yelling and running to the cabin with a black bear racing behind him. Jill got the gun but she couldn't shoot because her husband was running in front of the bear. Luckily Jack tripped on a tree root and fell down, giving Jill a clear shot. She shot the bear in the neck. Jill saved the shell, put a hole in it, and strung it over their bedpost, just to remind Jack how important she was in his life.

Other pioneer women told similar love stories. Laurel Tyrrell had met Rick, "the man of her dreams," when she had come to Alaska on an adventure and entered imaginatively into his frontier romance. Pam Haskin would never have gone to Alaska but for her husband Jeff and his dream of homesteading and hunting in the wilderness. Hers was at bedrock a story of sacrifice that she had romanced into an inspirational parable in her book *A Deliberate Life*, each chapter describing an ordeal in the wilderness and the moral lesson she learned from it.

The pioneer women's narratives downplayed the great love stories that had brought them to Central. They were well aware of the stigma that contemporary society placed on women who followed their man and were "nothing more" than mothers. "Happy Loser," a poem of one of the pioneer women, captured the tension between the narrative of success and the narrative of failure competing for her own interpretation of her life story.

Pam Haskin snowshoeing in the wilderness. Courtesy Pam Haskin.

Laurel Tyrrell and her baby, Jacob, at their trapline cabin on Birch Creek, 1983. This image, mother with baby, is a classic motif of the frontier romance. Courtesy Laurel Tyrrell.

> Packed up my camper
> Gonna travel around
> Have to get out of this crowded town
> Just not a career girl
> (to my parents' dismay)
> Prefer the pioneer life
> I'll find a way . . .
> Took the road north
> Drove the Alcan
> Got Lucky I know
> I found a good friend.

The original poem contained the line "I found a good man." The word *man* had the not inconsiderable poetic advantage of rhyming with "Alcan." But the writer did not want friends in the Lower 48 to read that line and think ill of her. The friends of her youth remained her reference

After their "Daniel Boone" period, Laurel Tyrrell and her husband Rick built themselves a new house in Central, peeling the logs with the help of their neighbors. The
Tyrrells' lives follow the seasons. When this picture was taken, they were hunting at
their fall moose camp. Courtesy Andrew Kleinfeld.

group, her imaginary audience for the story of her life. The poem moves
to its final stanzas, defiant, the lines and her life narrative firm in the
story frame of the pioneer romance:

> Wouldn't trade that old scrub spruce
> Not even the bugs
> For life with the traffic,
> Cement buildings and thugs
> Home for me now
> Is this remote northern place
> Thank you God
> I finally lost the rat race!

The Significance of the Pioneer Women's Frontier Romance

Let us return to the two questions with which this chapter began: Why did these pioneer women choose to go into the wilderness and live such difficult lives, not only without the conveniences most women take for granted but even without basic medical care for their babies should an emergency strike? And why did Kay Mero express the hope we would never be without these mythic figures?

Most of the women settled in Central because they had met a good man and joined in his frontier romance. But they were not bit players in these men's stories. The pioneer women wrote scripts of their own. Their public story was a romance about a pioneer community where they lived out a nostalgic version of the American frontier past. Their public story cast them as heroines displaying courage and competence, who had mastered skills like killing bears (traditionally the province of males), and who had made wise choices about what values to live by.

Their personal stories were more layered and conflicted, but these narratives were agentic stories, not victimization stories. Living in the Alaska wilderness gave them unique source material for authoring their lives. Few other women in contemporary America homesteaded or lived on homesites where they had to use a dogsled in the winter or a boat in summer to get to their front door. The wilderness women wove their own frontier romances, both narratives of redemption and narratives of construction of a heroic identity.

Their audience of friends and family applauded these life stories, listening avidly to adventure tales about living in the Alaska wilderness, when the women visited them in the Lower 48. Even parents who had first criticized their daughters' choices to live in Alaska came to take pride in what they had made of their lives. Parents sometimes saw their children as carrying on the family tradition of pioneering, recounted in cherished family narratives. Pam Haskin now gets asked the question her own great-grandfather was asked when he went pioneering at the turn of the nineteenth century, settling in Texas: "Every person I meet back here wants to know how you people live so far from civilization."

Americans cherish the frontier romance and love to see our collective story enacted. We reward these dream merchants. After "Jack and Jill" built their storybook cabin in the wilderness, they made an upsetting discovery. They had accidentally built their cabin on federal land and had to move off. They searched frantically for a private parcel of land nearby to which they could move their cabin. Finally, they located such a piece of land, owned by an old man who lived in Kentucky. He wasn't going to sell his piece of the Alaska dream to anybody. He had been approached before. But hearing their story, he decided to make them a "crazy little deal." They could move their cabin onto his property, rent-free, if they would come down to Kentucky every other year and give him a slide show of their life in the wilderness. For the next twenty years, the old man got his frontier theater. When he died at 96, he willed the property to them.

The wilderness women had paradoxically stepped out of and maintained traditional female roles. They had achieved the same kind of successes as had the men who lived out the frontier romance. Their personal narratives featured their own growth and achievements—the development of talents they never knew they had. They too saw themselves as the heroines of the monomyth, returning with a message that would revive the community: You too can still set out for a new world, take the risk, and achieve your own wild dreams.

CHAPTER 3

....

The Frontier Romance as Mask

The mask misdirects society as it protects the masker. The masker
assumes a disguise that attempts to divert society by deception or
satisfy it by simulating an ideal.

—Susan Harris Smith, *Masks in Modern Drama*

This chapter explores the use of the frontier narrative as mask, camouflage, and disguise. In its benign form, a psychologically disordered
but harmless individual embraces frontier symbols and imagery—bushy
beard, cabin, wilderness tent at forty degrees below zero—in an effort to
create a dignified identity, to become an iconic symbol. Such a frontier
poseur gains freedom from social demands he cannot fulfill, a sooth-
ing solitude, and time to heal. The frontier identity becomes a form of
self-medication, an effort to create a narrative of the self that rescripts a
disordered life story into a heroic narrative of rebellion from convention.

In its malignant form, the frontier poseur suffers from serious mental
illness and in some cases is a dangerous psychopath. These men use the
imagery and symbols of the frontier to camouflage their psychopathology
and to divert society from the dangers they pose.[1] The person assumes a
familiar identity, just another would-be mountain man, just another end-
of-the-roader. Eventually, his psychopathology breaks out of the costume,
creating disaster for the community that harbors him.

An obscure research paper from Australia offers an illuminating perspective on this phenomenon. In "Flight into the Wilderness as a Psychiatric Syndrome," J. E. Cawte, a psychiatrist who served as superintendent of

Enfield Hospital in South Australia, examines the psychiatric disturbances in over a hundred cases of people who went into Australia's outback.[2] "The motivations of people who are drawn to the remaining frontiers of the world range from the adventurously realistic to the patently psychotic with infinite gradations in between," Cawte concludes. "'Eccentricity,' 'robust individualism,' 'troppo' are local labels for such people, any word except 'mental illness' which is taboo."[3]

In the Alaska vernacular, such sad characters are assigned the social identity "end-of-the-roaders." Disheveled and disorganized, some become fodder for sad but amusing local stories. In Central, people tell the tale of the wannabe trapper who came up with the idea of placing knives in a stream to kill the seals when they come up for air. In Nome, people describe a deranged young wanderer who planned to walk across the Bering Sea ice to Siberia. In Fairbanks, a minister tells the story of a couple he sheltered in his church, who told him they were on their way to a wilderness trapping cabin: "The guy wanted to get away from it all, he was feeling the lure of the North, he saw himself as Nikki, Wild Dog of the North." He refused the minister's offer of a parka for the woman. She didn't need a parka, he said, because she wouldn't be leaving the cabin all winter. The minister persuaded the woman not to accompany him. That winter the man committed suicide.

The mountain man costume, so familiar to Alaskans, does not cue the audience to the threat these individuals present. "We tolerate and treat as neighbors some very odd people," said one young woman living in Talkeetna. "One of my neighbors has a giant gun collection. It's his passion. We accept it. Because so many lives are unconventional, he fits in." The historical tolerance of a frontier society for strange individuals without a legible past is the sociological reality that makes such masking effective. Such figures seem to their audience just colorful actors in the theater of the frontier, contributing to the collective frontier romance people enjoy seeing performed. These frontier characters reassure nostalgic Alaskans that the state is still "The Last Frontier."

While some individuals use the frontier identity as a bid for respect, in other instances the audience projects its own frontier romance upon them. Whenever I drive down the Alaska Highway, for example, I look for the battered green school bus where a skinny, alcoholic Vietnam veteran who calls himself "Jedediah" displays fantastic chainsaw art made from diamond willow. Dressed in green fatigues and black boots without laces, he lives in a waterless shack in the woods. He forages for wood for his art—sculptures of frightening eagles clutching salmon in their talons, disturbing skulls and skeletons, and diamond willow bowls and tables of odd and innovative design. He doesn't deal well with society, his daughter tells me. He is something of an outlaw who came to Alaska in search of nature, spirituality, and Indians. My husband and I buy his diamond willow bowls, coffee tables, and eagle sculptures because we enjoy surrounding ourselves with what we interpret as the symbols of the frontier. They are the props of our own frontier romance.

The folklore of Alaska contains numerous tales of odd characters, loners, and misfits who helped create the dramatic ethos of the frontier.[4] "Nimrod," for example, gained fame as the man who shot a bear, constructed dentures using the bear's teeth, and then ate the bear with the animal's own teeth.[5] "He used spruce pitch to make the impressions, sheep teeth for the four front teeth, caribou teeth back of those, and bear teeth for the molars," writes Elva Scott about this legendary character. Erwin A. Robertson hailed from a distinguished Scottish family and headed over the Chilkoot Pass in 1898, dreaming of building a flying machine. According to local lore, Nimrod could make anything but a living.

Another such colorful character, Billy Gates, lived alone for twenty-five years on his mining claim in Livengood, building a stockade around his house and garden, and raising a white flag when he wanted to communicate with people.[6] He walked into Livengood "with yellow snags for teeth, a flour sack lined with bunny fur for his hat, his pants stitched with willow strips, constantly mumbling about Purgatory and the Promised Land up near the Crazy Mountains."[7]

While some of those who don the costume of the frontier or have the role thrust upon them add to the richness and diversity of life in Alaska, this is not always the case. In the sections below, I first describe examples of the frontier narrative functioning as camouflage for crime. I then describe an example of the frontier narrative used harmlessly as a healing narrative for psychological disturbance, succeeding at self-medication.

The Frontier Romance as Camouflage for Mental Illness

MICHAEL SILKA

Michael Silka styled himself as a "mountain man from Chicago."[8] As a teenager, he would walk around the Chicago suburb of Hoffman Estates with primed muzzle-loading rifles. He was arrested twice in Illinois for weapons offenses. "All he wanted to do was to get enough money to be independent and live in the wilderness," said his high school teacher after the tragedy.

A hotel owner in Manitoba said that Silka always had six or seven rifles and shotguns lying on the seat of his car: "His favorite was obviously a Rolling Block, a modern replica of a single-shot, large-caliber rifle used originally on the American frontier."

Michael Silka, who called himself a "mountain man," killed seven people in the remote village of Manley Hot Springs. Since he looked like so many other bush-haired drifters who styled themselves mountain men, the Manley community did not recognize that Silka was a serial killer. Courtesy *Fairbanks Daily News-Miner*.

In 1984, Silka moved into Hopkinsville, a cluster of cabins at the edge of the interior city of Fairbanks. His neighbor Roger Culp disappeared, the first sign of trouble. When troopers came to investigate the blood spots near Silka's cabin door, Silka said he had been washing the blood from moose hides. The troopers came back with a warrant to search the shack, later identifying the spots as human blood. By this time Silka had disappeared.

Driving his old brown Dodge, Silka made a run for Manley Hot Springs, a frontier fantasy of a town in the wilderness with a graceful steel bridge spanning the creek, log cabins, flower boxes filled with petunias and pansies, and a roadhouse with windows of antique glass dating back to 1907. Silka seemed weird to the Manley folk, talking about smelling clams in six feet of water.[9] But the people of Manley had seen a lot of drifters, and Silka didn't seem any different from the other bushy-haired characters who arrived with big talk about staking a homestead on the Zitziana River. He looked like he was in better shape than many of them, talking about using his military service to get bonus points for staking free land.

Silka made camp down by the boat launch, about a quarter mile out of town. People who went down there suddenly started to disappear. The pregnant Joyce Klein went down to the boat launch with her husband and two-year-old son Marshall. The family never returned. Nor did Joe McVey and his friend Dale Madajski, who had gone down to launch McVey's boat. Nor did Albert Hagen Jr., who drove his pickup down to the boat launch. An Athabascan trapper, Fred Burk, motored down the river to Manley Hot Springs from his camp and did not return.

When the neighbors went down to the boat landing to investigate, Silka had disappeared. Afraid Silka too might be among the missing, they called his auto license number into the police. The license plate turned up the name of "Michael Silka," wanted for the murder of Roger Culp. By the time the state troopers arrived, Silka had gotten far up the Zitziana River in the boat he had stolen from Fred Burk. Silka sought a movie shoot-out with the troopers and he chose his ground well. Protecting his back with the trees, Silka figured that anyone coming in to get him would have to appear in front of him, coming in from flat, open ground. When a helicopter with state troopers arrived, Silka stepped out from

When two helicopters with armed troopers closed in on Silka, he stepped out from behind a tree and opened fire, killing one trooper instantly and wounding another. Another trooper aimed with care and fired. Silka lay dead, his head in the river. This picture shows the troopers bringing back Silka's body. Courtesy *Fairbanks Daily News-Miner.*

behind a tree and opened fire. Two shots hit the Bell 206B helicopter, almost bringing it down, missing the control lines by inches. Silka killed one trooper and wounded another. Trooper Jeff Hall took aim with his M-16 and killed Silka.

Silka had killed nine people. Three bodies, including the pregnant Joyce Klein and her small son Marshall, were never recovered from the river. Before coming to Alaska, Silka had no record of violence. Perhaps he had committed violent acts and was not caught. But the frontier ethos of Alaska may have amplified his violent tendencies. Just as the frontier romance provides a script for opportunity ("go west, young man"), the frontier romance provides a script for violence, such as Silka's gunfight with the troopers.

PAPA PILGRIM AND HIS PIONEER FAMILY

Papa Pilgrim looks like a Biblical patriarch, with his flowing white beard, his eyes focused on the distance, on a Promised Land. Standing by his side in the carefully posed family picture is his wife, whom he named "Country Rose," and they are surrounded by their fifteen children. One grown son, Joshua, wears a hand-tooled leather hat with his faded flannel red shirt and worn jeans. Four other adult sons guard the family, standing like pillars on the sides. At their feet sit the smallest daughters, Bethlehem, Lamb, and Psalms, with blonde hair and bare feet twisting under their long country dresses. The family could have stepped right out of a western movie set, and this is indeed the portrait they are trying to project. Dressed in pioneer costume, growing vegetables in their large garden, hunting their own meat, baking homemade bread and cookies on an old kitchen stove, and creating gospel bluegrass music, the Pilgrim family is reenacting the stock story, in its movie version, of a pioneer family in the West. Each member of the family plays a bluegrass instrument. "They are the real thing. They are genuine," raved Billy Oskay, who recorded their album at Portland's Big Red Studio, when they brought their son to Portland for medical treatment.

The Pilgrim family fooled western historians. "Folks, if you have an opportunity to look at this website TODAY, DO IT!" wrote Sam Matthews-Lamb, a historian who managed a listserv for other western historians. "It's an amazing story of modern-day frontier folk battling the federal government. This story would be a great resource for a course on the American West," he enthused.

"Why do you see the family as ringers for western pioneers?" I asked him. He obligingly listed the qualities that in the mind of a western historian linked the Pilgrim family to nineteenth-century western pioneers:

- Fiercely individualistic
- Often highly religious (if family unit)
- Lives off the land and is largely self-sufficient
- Music plays key role in their cultural/social upbringing
- Head-to-head with governmental control

Papa Pilgrim leads a few of his children in gospel and bluegrass tunes before bedtime at the cabin. The family purchased its instruments from pawn shops and drew lots from Papa Pilgrim's old leather mountain hat to see who would play the banjo, the dobro, the mandolin, the fiddle, and the bass fiddle. They have cut an album of their homespun mountain gospel, *Alaska's Pilgrim Family Minstrels, Put My Name Down*. While many outsiders see them as frontier frauds, specialists see the Pilgrims' gospel bluegrass as authentic folk music untainted by the commercial world. Courtesy *Anchorage Daily News*.

Papa Pilgrim was going head-to-head in a fight with the National Park Service. In Alaska, every resident gets a dividend check from the oil taxes the state receives, passed through Alaska's Permanent Fund. With a seventeen-member family, Papa Pilgrim had $30,000 in Permanent Fund dividends to put a down payment on an old mine, an inholding in the Wrangell–St. Elias National Park. He called his domain "Hillbilly Heaven"—a 420-acre property, fourteen miles up a glacial creek from the wilderness town of McCarthy. When Papa Pilgrim ran a Caterpillar D4 tractor through the old mining road so he could bring in building materials and winter supplies, the family became a political symbol in a battle between the National Park Service, upholding wilderness protection, and the American Land Rights Association, upholding private property rights. For the media, Papa Pilgrim forged a pioneer drama, casting his family as neighborly folk bringing home-baked cookies to the National Park Service officials trying to prevent his access to his land.

But their pioneer fantasy at Hillbilly Heaven was just a costume change. Before coming to Alaska, the family had lived out the hippie romance, moving from Haight-Ashbury to the Sangre de Cristo Mountains, where the man who now calls himself "Papa Pilgrim" then called himself "Sunstar." Born Robert Hale, the son of an All-American football star, he eloped with the daughter of John B. Connally, later the governor of Texas, when she was sixteen years old. According to Hale's version of the story, his young wife committed suicide in a hotel room, firing a gun into her own face, while he was trying to wrest the gun from her hands.

After marrying two other women with whom he had children, Hale married another sixteen-year-old, Kurina Rose Besler, the mother of his fifteen children, and moved them to Hillbilly Heaven. Becoming a born-again Christian, Hale transformed himself into Papa Pilgrim, Kurina into Country Rose, and renamed those children whose previous names did not fit the stage name requirements for his new story line. His daughter "Butterfly," for example, was renamed "Elizabeth." In Alaska, they lived out the script of a pioneer family in the wilderness. Many who saw them were enchanted by the tableau and offered them their services in their fight with the National Park Service or help in meeting the family's needs for food and clothing.

Papa Pilgrim claimed that his children lived under careful supervision. By his decree, Pilgrim girls could not shake hands. No child could go anywhere unless accompanied by another family member. The children all bathed fully clothed and have never seen, he claimed, a naked body. Then one of the older sons found out his father was committing incest with one of his small sisters in a cabin on the property. The young man turned his father in. Papa Pilgrim was arrested after twelve days on the run, charged with thirty felonies for rape, assault, and incest, and was sentenced to fourteen years in prison for sexually abusing his daughter. The shattered family abandoned the name "Pilgrim" and found refuge with a Christian homesteading family that had nine children of its own living in a log home outside Palmer.

Papa Pilgrim, his wife, Country Rose, and their fifteen children came to Alaska from New Mexico, settling on an inholding in Wrangell–St. Elias National Park. The Pilgrims' pioneer narrative conflicts with the wilderness narrative of environmentalists. After the Pilgrims bulldozed a trail to their inholding down an old mining road, the battle between the two narratives was on. Many saw the Pilgrims as inauthentic frontier frauds who were desecrating one of the greatest natural wonders of the world. Courtesy Laurent Granier and Philippe Lansac.

Papa Pilgrim and his family were impostors, using the symbols of the frontier romance to mislead their audience. As their sad narrative unfolded, the national media no longer referred to him as "Papa Pilgrim" but as "Robert Hale," who sang and whimpered at his trial, a man who took his family into the wilderness where he could commit horrific acts of incest. Their play was over.

The Frontier Romance as a Healing Narrative

Other psychologically disturbed individuals who present themselves as frontier characters pose no such danger to others. They use the frontier romance as a form of narrative therapy, a self-help effort to script a story that gives their lives glamour and meaning. The frontier romance with its stock wilderness characters provides them with a ready-made identity through which they can achieve dignity in their own eyes and respect in the eyes of others. Through the frontier romance, they turn messy lives into art. Living in the wilderness, without the pressures of other people and the demands of regular work, some find relief from their disturbance and, after awhile, emerge from their solitary lives with greater psychic balance.

"STORYKNIFE SAM"

Storyknife Sam is a sinewy bearded man who lives in a double-wall tent in the forest in winter, with only his three dogs for company. He looks like a character from a frontier film. So he has been. He was an extra in the film of Jack London's *White Fang* and proudly shows me his scrapbook with glossy photographs. "I was the most photographed extra on the set. Good for the ego," he says. He grew up playing Davy Crockett and watching Walt Disney on television. "I still live in Frontierland," he says. "Everyone thinks I have an easy life because I don't have a job. I work really hard to maintain a life of doing nothing out in the woods."

An auto body repairman for twenty years in Oklahoma, Storyknife Sam left home and wandered. "I wasn't the same after I got out of the Navy," he tells me, searching for some explanation for his problems. "I kept moving farther and farther north until I got to Alaska. I fit right in here. I don't have a shower or wash my clothes for six months, but I just got my dogs and they don't notice." His high cackling laughs pierce the tape-recorded interview, erupting at odd moments, for no apparent reason.

"A lot of people think I'm crazy, like my brother and my mother do," he says. "But my brother envies me because I have a free life. Once he said, 'Maybe you're not crazy after all.'"

To make enough money to feed himself and his dogs in the wilderness, he carves "story knives" for tourists. Eskimo children used such story knives to draw illustrations in the snow when they told stories to each other. He searches the woods for just the right pieces of willow and sits by the river carving and polishing the handles, first using 40-grit sandpaper and then using 1000-grit sandpaper to make them gleam. He sells his story knives at bazaars, each priced at about $200. As a source of more reliable cash, he makes cheap cottonwood plaques as well, with hooks of salmon vertebrae wrapped with spruce roots. The plaques carry inspirational messages from such philosophers as Thoreau: "Why should we live with such hurry and waste of life?"

When I last heard from Storyknife Sam, he had left the woods and gone to Skagway. His story knives are now featured in Alaska art galleries. Other wilderness eccentrics contribute extraordinary art, like Vladimar Vinitzki, whose communion with his cherished family of dogs enabled him to take photographs that capture the spirit, movement, and pure joy of sled dogs when they race. Such idiosyncratic figures add to the richness and color of life in Alaska and validate the state's romance with the frontier.

Many of these misfits contribute in another odd way—by bringing out the best in other people. Storyknife Sam found a veterinarian to sew up his dogs for virtually no cost after they got into a fight. Jedediah lives on land rent-free from the generosity of the owner of a local enterprise, who sells his sculptures and looks after him. People took in Country Rose and her small children after Papa Pilgrim was arrested. People are generous to these frontier icons. The audience of this frontier theater gets a psychic return, the satisfaction of seeing the frontier story enacted, like a bedtime story that can never be too often told.

These men—and they are virtually all men—use the frontier romance to give meaning to their lives. They cannot deal with the pressures and tasks of human communities. Some of them, like Michael Silka and Papa Pilgrim, are evil and dangerous. Others, like Storyknife Sam and Jedidiah, are misfits and eccentrics who do not threaten others. Quite the contrary, this second group brings enjoyment to other people through their artwork and the frontier theater that their lives create. Both groups play with the mountain man persona, but they bear no resemblance to nineteenth-century mountain men.

CHAPTER 4

··

The Pioneers of the Spirit

A map of the world that does not include Utopia is not worth even glancing at, for it leaves out the one country at which humanity is always landing.

—Oscar Wilde, "The Soul of Man under Socialism"

Narrative offers an imaginative framework for more than the creation of the identity of individuals. Narratives can seize the imagination of an entire group of people and create a distinctive community identity. The wilderness women in Central wove together the story of themselves as an early American pioneer settlement, keeping alive the virtues of community, of neighborliness and mutual aid, in an isolated, harsh environment. In this chapter, I describe how another group of people used a different variation of the frontier romance—the Pilgrims coming to the New World to practice their religious beliefs—to create a "city on a hill" in the wilderness in Alaska. The important point from the perspective of narrative psychology is that the narrative is not used to fashion a community identity in retrospect. The community narrative drives a quest. Two stories came to life in the communal narrative of Whitestone Farms: the frontier narrative of the journey to a new land and the narrative of the early Christians living in a communal society.

In Alaska, these versions of the frontier romance are enacted in a cluster of religious communities, Whitestone Farms, Eagles' Ridge, Dry Creek, and New Hope, hidden in the wilderness, in small towns, on unmarked spur roads off the Alaska Highway. I focus on the largest, fastest-growing, and most prosperous community. The people of Whitestone Farms caravanned across the United States from New Hampshire to Alaska and built with the labor of their own hands not only a city on a hill but an actual city, with a tabernacle, housing, farms, a dairy, workshops, plumbing, and electricity.

The Pilgrim narrative is one plot line in their community romance, a source of emotionally resonant scenes and imagery, which places what they are doing in the symbolic context of the American founding. When the Pilgrims came to Plymouth, their purpose was to found a new Jerusalem, where people could live in the ways that they thought God wanted them to live. The people of Whitestone Farms made a similar pilgrimage, not from England but from New England, and they were trying to do a similar thing. What is remarkable is how well they succeeded. The community is still in existence and was thriving in 2009, more than a quarter of a century after its founding.

The Pilgrim story is one source of scenes and characters for their community romance. But the narrative energy driving Whitestone Farms comes from another story, Acts 4:32, which describes the beginnings of the church in the communal way of life of the earliest Christians: "And the congregation of those who believed were of one heart and soul; and not one of them claimed that anything belonging to him was his own, but all things were common property to them." Whitestone Farms fashioned itself in the image of the earliest Christian communities where people lived in small communal groups, sharing what they had, and awaiting the return of Christ. Whitestone Farms sees itself as just such a charismatic community—independent, nondenominational, a spiritual remnant. They are "building an ark" where they can escape the materialistic, self-centered society around them and raise their children to honor spiritual values. The American frontier for hundreds of years has been stage and setting for such spiritual quests.

Utopian Versions of the American Frontier Romance

In the American imagination, the West has always represented a realm of dramatic possibility. No quest could be more magnificent or more fantastic than the quest to create a new and more perfect society.[1] Ideal societies have always existed in the human imagination—the Garden of Eden, the City of God, Homer's Elysian Fields, El Dorado, Shangri-La, Mount Mero of Hindu lore. Sir Thomas Moore coined the term *utopia* (a clever wordplay in the Greek, signifying at once "no place" and "good place") in his description of an imaginary island off the coast of America, free from the evils of contemporary England. The utopian dream takes a multitude of forms, each version correcting the particular faults of the society of the time. Thus, European peasants dreamed of "The Land of Cockaigne" where the seas were made of wine, roasted birds dropped from the sky, and those who labored were arrested. Edward Bellamy in his utopian novel *Looking Backward*, published in 1888, highlights the social evils of capitalism and transports his hero to a socialist new world where people are allotted work based on their abilities and are paid the same stipend of $4,000 a year. Bellamy's novel (the second best-selling novel of the nineteenth century, after *Uncle Tom's Cabin*) spawned hundreds of "Bellamy societies" in the United States.

In America, this utopian literature turned into life. "Here the social dreams of the Old World were dreams no longer, but things of flesh and blood," writes Arthur Bestor, describing the amazement of European visitors who observed and wrote about the communal societies dotting the northern and western regions of America.[2] A wild variety of utopian communities—religious, politico-economic, psychosocial—took form on American soil. "Not a reading man but has a draft of a new community in his waistcoat pocket," wrote Ralph Waldo Emerson to his great friend Carlyle in the early nineteenth century. Religious communal societies existed in America for a hundred years before the country was founded. The first was Plockhoy's Mennonite Commonwealth started on the shores of the Delaware River in 1663. A great wave of voluntary societies swept across America in the 1840s, fashioned as refuges from the smoky cities, toil, and insecurities spawned by the Industrial Revolution. At the time of the Civil War, the Shakers numbered some six thousand men and women in spiritual communities stretching from Hancock, Massachusetts, to Pleasant Hill, Kentucky.

The utopian narratives of Europe became actual communities in America for three reasons important to the frontier, not only as a geographic

place but also as an idea. America symbolized a fresh start, a new beginning, "a new order of the ages." The idea that America has a God-inspired
mission to be a beacon of hope, an exemplar for other societies, is the theme,
resonating for almost four hundred years, of John Winthrop's speech to the
Puritan company crossing the Atlantic to found the Massachusetts Bay
Colony: "We must consider that we shall be a City Upon a Hill, the eyes of
all people are upon us." The idea of such special purpose remains deeply
embedded in America's collective consciousness.

Second, new societies require large tracts of cheap land, which the
American frontier offered. In 1825, the Welsh-born industrialist and phi-
lanthropist Robert Owen, for example, established his model socialist
society, New Harmony, in America rather than Great Britain because he
could purchase a huge parcel of thirty thousand acres of land in Indiana.
He bought the land for his socialist society from another utopian group,
the Harmonists, who themselves had gone to Indiana in search of a large
tract of cheap land where they could build their own communal society.
Like many other intentional societies, New Harmony disintegrated, dis-
solving within two years over disagreements about ideology, religion,
and social arrangements, along with personal jealousies, incompetence,
and malingering.

Third, utopian societies were established on the American frontier
because such sparsely populated territory offered distance from critical
eyes and more freedom from social censure and interference. Some of
these experimental societies shocked the surrounding society. The Mormons trekked to Utah, where they could practice polygamy. The most
radical society was Oneida, founded by John Humphrey Noyes in 1848
and lasting until 1880. Oneida practiced "complex marriage" in which
every man in the community was considered married to every woman
in the community, and no two people could have a "selfish" exclusive
relationship. Noyes created a eugenics program, featuring "male conti-
nence" in which a man could not ejaculate within a woman unless he had
been selected by the community to breed. Community doctrine included
"ascending fellowship" through which the powerful members of the community became spiritual guides to younger members. Older males not
unexpectedly chose to be the spiritual mentors of young female virgins.

Most of these utopian experiments soon perished or, like the Mormons, evolved into less radical forms. Religious communities, bound together by spiritual commitments, tended to last longer. Amana, a spiritual community much like Whitestone Farms, survived for eighty-nine years. The Shakers, famous for their dancing, whirling, and other ecstatic forms of worship, are still in existence even though the communities practiced celibacy and strictly segregated men and women. One Shaker community, founded in 1783, can be found in Sabbathday Lake, Maine. While other community ventures have occurred in Alaska, with varying degrees of communal living, and varying rationales, only the religious societies have lasted for long periods of time. That not only individuals but also whole groups of people could start all over again and create more perfect societies is one of the great legends of American life.

Constructing a Narrative of Separation

I had lived in Alaska for close to thirty years, but I had no idea, nor did most other Alaskans, that a network of religious communities existed in Alaska. I visited the community, sent my adolescent children to live with their teenagers, and invited the people of Whitestone Farms to my home. I conducted interviews with members of the community, recording their life histories and exploring why they had come to Alaska and built this city in the wilderness. This is, to my knowledge, the only study of the charismatic religious communities in Alaska.

Whitestone Farms is not on the map, nor on the road system. The community lies across the Delta River and can be reached only by boat in summer and by an ice road the community builds to cross the river in winter. You must be guided in to this spiritual hideout. I had come across the community by accident, learning of their location when I was visiting one of their highway businesses, Rika's Roadhouse, a tourist attraction. I asked a salesperson if I could do research on this unusual northern community, the community agreed to the research project, and I was guided in. I was frightened as I drove over the ice road in the darkness of winter at midday, following the orange taillights of a battered old truck. Driving a thirty-five-hundred-pound Jeep over a frozen ice river is risky—your car could plunge through the ice, trapping you in freezing water. Dark, twisted driftwood lay tangled on the ice. Suddenly I saw scrub brush. I had reached the other side. The lights of Whitestone Farms blinked in the darkness.

The year was 1994, one year after the federal Bureau of Alcohol, Tobacco, and Firearms had tried to enter the compound of a cult, the Branch Davidians at Waco, to execute an arrest warrant on the cult leader, David Koresh, and to search the premises for illegal firearms and explosives. After a fifty-one-day standoff, federal agents had rammed the Davidian compound with tanks, punching holes in the walls to throw in tear gas, creating a fire, the very Armageddon the cult had prophesied. The fire killed eighty members of the cult. Stories can be damaged or turned

Bill Grier, the spiritual leader of Whitestone Farms, looks out over the Tanana River, the Richardson Highway, and the Trans-Alaska Pipeline. Wild in his youth, Bill Grier had a spiritual revelation driving on a California highway, as did Saul on the road to Damascus. Bill Grier says he wishes he had been called to bring the community to someplace warmer than Delta Junction, Alaska. Courtesy *Anchorage Daily News*.

into perverse forms, the utopian tale transformed into the actuality of a dangerous cult in the thrall of a messianic leader. Entering Whitestone Farms, I worried about what I was getting into.

I arrived at the tabernacle, a great cedar building with floor-to-ceiling windows framing the Alaska Range. Bette Grier, the wife of the founder of Whitestone Farms, swung open the heavy doors of the tabernacle to greet me. I was astonished to see this elegant woman, wearing open-toed high heels, her skirt a swirl of black silk, with understated makeup, her ash blonde hair gathered into a sleek knot. "God's bait"—that's what her husband, Bill Grier, called her. She had grown up the daughter of Presbyterian missionaries who had gone to South America.

Bill Grier, the religious leader of Whitestone Farms, was in his sixties, muscular, with silvering hair, radiating vitality and restless energy. Bill Grier looked like the fit Californian he once had been. He had lived

In the summer, boating across the Delta River is the only way to reach Whitestone Farms. In the winter, the community is accessible only by an ice road. The community sought isolation in Alaksa from the countercultural values that swept over America during the 1960s. Courtesy Judy Ferguson.

The community of Whitestone Farms sits down and eats together at the tabernacle, the center of communal life. The tables are set with cloth tablecloths and napkins in carved napkin rings, and most of the food comes from the gardens, bakery, and dairy at the farm. Bill and Betty Grier live upstairs in a single room, sharing a bathroom with another couple. At Whitestone, renunciation means ridding the soul of selfishness, not doing without worldly pleasures. Courtesy *Anchorage Daily News*.

a wild life in California, devoted to horse racing, real estate, and surfing. Driving on the freeway one day, he started shaking and speaking in tongues. He pulled over to the side of the road and called a friend, a psychiatrist: Was he having a mental breakdown? Yes, that could be happening, but there were other interpretations of this experience. Bill Grier interpreted what was happening to him in a narrative framework, a Biblical story. The Lord was calling him on a California freeway, as the Lord had called Paul on the road to Damascus. His grandmother had always told him he was going to be a preacher. Spiritually aggressive, he committed symbolic acts of insurrection: in Boston, he set up pans of soapy water and washed the American flag in public to make it clean.

Bill and Bette Grier looked like no people I had ever seen in Alaska bush country, and the men and women crowded in the tabernacle waiting for dinner looked equally strange. Most women who live in the Alaska bush, like the pioneer women of Central, saw freedom from fashion as one of the benefits of their frontier lives. The women of Whitestone Farms were no "bush babes" in faded blue jeans and washed-out sweatshirts, without makeup. The women of Whitestone Farms had dressed for dinner, wearing dresses and perfume, eyeliner, mascara, and lipstick.

None of the men sported a bushy "Alaska beard," one symbol of men who lived in the Alaska wilderness. Nor were the men wearing standard wilderness dress, rumpled work shirts and old blue jeans. The men too had dressed for dinner, replacing their work clothes with pressed slacks and fresh shirts. They were all clean-shaven. The men at Whitestone Farms had made the decision to shave their faces clean, a sign that they were wiping the slate clean, a symbol that they were not in a spiritual state of rebellion.

What did their appearance signify? Separatism. Nancy Porter, who came to Whitestone with the first group of pilgrims in 1982, emphasized the significance of such dress in a paper she wrote for a university sociology class: "Another aspect of our life together which separates us from life outside is dress standards. While this might not have been an issue 30 years ago, it is very noticeable today where virtually no standard exists. I mention it simply because when parents or other visitors come, it seems to be the first thing noticed.

"The intent for women to wear dresses or skirts instead of pants is that we believe men and women are different and should look different. Our wearing of dresses comes against the unisex look and takes a stand against punk styles designed to denigrate men and women and reduce both sexes to a low level of homogeneousness."

Looking over the tabernacle, I was astonished to see tables formally set for eight with white tablecloths. At each person's place lay a hand-carved birch napkin ring enclosing a white cloth napkin. Four young women stood formally in front of the kitchen, announcing the menu and saying they hoped the community would enjoy the homemade food: roast, mashed potatoes, broccoli, salad, and apple pie. Much of the food was grown on the farm. A server from each table rose to get the meal. One member of the community played dinner music on a grand piano. After Starbucks coffee, a luxury the community permitted itself, one person from each table went back to the kitchen for dishpans of soapy water, rinse water, and dishtowels. Men as well as women did the dishes.

Did this formal dinner mark a special occasion? Not at all. The community ate most meals together. White lace tablecloths, cloth napkins, and napkin rings were features of every meal, symbols of standards within as well as without.

"Everyone is gathered together three times a day, and there is occasion to be one. With so many activities going on in so many places, it is essential that there are times during the day when our focus and hearts can be drawn together again," Nancy Porter wrote. "Acts 2 tells of the early church 'continually devoting themselves to the apostles' teaching, and to fellowship, to the breaking of bread and to prayer.'"

Whitestone Farms numbered about 180 people, and most were young couples with several children. People sat down to dinner in families, parents with babies in high chairs and sometimes three or four young children. Once children turned eighteen, they sat apart from their families. Table seatings were rotated to prevent the formation of factions, whose quarrels could undermine community life.

The maintenance of communal life also required strict controls on sexuality. "Walking it out," was what Whitestone Farms called its courtship customs. "Walking the plank," was what the young people called it. The custom was designed to make it possible for couples to court and to break up and still live together in community. When two people "feel the Lord would like them to become better acquainted[,] with the possibility of marriage, they submit the relationship to the elders for prayer, and they begin to 'walk it out,'" explained Nancy Porter. "They cannot touch each other (although the elders turn a blind eye to a bit of friendly hugging and cheek kissing that goes no farther). But they are placed together at meals and religious services and they spend a lot of time talking. Most couples walk it out for a year before they marry."

Whitestone Farms is part of a loose association of "wilderness" farms that had originally been started by followers of Sam Fife, who called himself "the light of the world" and called on his followers to prepare for the "fullness of time." The group started wilderness farms in Mississippi, South America, Canada, and Alaska. Most had disbanded by the end of the twentieth century. The communities that had survived were located primarily in regions with an ethos that supported the frontier romance, in Alaska and in Canada. The Peace River country of Canada, the setting of other such communities, had much in common with the Alaska frontier—open crown land, isolation, and an ethos of self-sufficiency. The religious communities in Alaska are independent, but they help each other out in emergencies or when specialized skills possessed by members of one community are needed in another community. The young adults in these small religious communities circulate among other communities, to search for compatible mates. Many young adults from other communities come to the college at Whitestone Farms.

Each religious community has a distinctive culture and its own criticism of the community down the road. Dry Creek, close to the Canadian border, started before Whitestone Farms in 1973, looks like an Amish community with its fields of horses, horse-drawn water wagons, and a cluster of log cabins. At the other extreme is a new community, Eagles' Ridge Ranch, a religious startup under Whitestone's "covering." Eagles' Ridge got its name from the eagles that congregated in one area of the land, swooping and floating down on thermal drafts of air, like surfers riding a wave. The community had just twenty-three people in 1995, and they were experimenting with different businesses, like raising Labrador dogs and running a trap-shooting club, to sustain the community and get money to build their tabernacle and communal housing. Mike Crouch, one of its elders, liked the thrill of starting new religious communities. He had been heavily into drugs when he graduated from college in the 1970s, moved to a religious community in Florida, then to one in Mississippi, and then to one in Alaska. A group got together, founded a new church, and bought a bankrupt farm. The financial base of Eagles' Ridge was the $45,000 a year that the community drew from the Conservation Reserve Program. The community was planting alternating rows of grass and trees, trying to bring back the wildlife.

How to earn enough money to support the religious community was a constant problem. Whitestone Farms had made the decision only to earn money through enterprises in which the members could work in community, in each others' company. Many other communal societies had fallen apart when individuals earned money outside the community and were then expected to contribute their earnings to the group.

Maintaining social harmony was a delicate business in a communal society. The woman who organized other women's work schedules had to
have the tact of a professional diplomat. Other communal societies in
Alaska had disintegrated when feuding families packed up and pulled
out. Whitestone Farms still had the cohesiveness born of a common origin, coming from the Church of the Living Word in New Hampshire. The
community does not proselytize. If someone had a "spiritual surge," as
Bill Grier put it, and wanted to join Whitestone Farms, Grier told him to
go to the church in New Hampshire first. Whitestone Farms supported
itself through running businesses like Rika's Roadhouse. The building
was falling apart when the community submitted a bid to the state of
Alaska to rebuild it and operate it for tourists. Theirs was the only bid.
Reconstructing Rika's Roadhouse cost the community close to $350,000
in materials and many months of labor. When the man heading up the
Rika's Roadhouse construction crew fell from the scaffolding onto the
concrete floor and lay unconscious for a week in the hospital, the "men
came together and filled in the gaps so completely it was impossible to
see a man was missing," wrote Nancy Porter. "I lost count of the nights I
greeted my husband and the rest of the men at the boat dock at midnight.
And yet they didn't return to the farm drained but invigorated. Rather
than fulfilling a building project, they were working together to fulfill
the will of God."

Whitestone Farms turned this historic site into a pioneer fantasy
with ducks, geese, and gardens of flowers and ornamental green cab-
bages that grew gigantic in the ceaseless daylight of an Alaska summer.
Rika's Roadhouse, selling meals and Whitestone crafts like diamond
willow tables, attracted over thirty thousand visitors a year. The community prospered, opening other businesses, such as a greenhouse that
sold plants in the summer, and a gas station and store on the highway.
A major business was a commercial cleaning company. Eight men from
Whitestone Farms drove a hundred miles into Fairbanks, where they
lived for a week at a time in a community house and cleaned office buildings during the night.

The income that Whitestone Farms receives from its businesses, after taxes and purchases, is held in common. The first ten percent is a
tithe, going to charitable causes outside the community. Ten percent of

the remaining income goes to a "family fund" that gives individuals a little personal spending money. Each person over the age of twelve gets one unit of this distribution, with the children getting half a unit. Personal inheritances and gifts belong to individuals.

Bill and Bette Grier, like everyone else in the community, have only one room to themselves, their bedroom. They share a bathroom with the couple who lives in the bedroom next to them. "When I came to Alaska and joined the community, I honestly thought about what I was giving up. My standard of living. My china," Bette Grier told me. "When you are pioneering something new, you don't know exactly what you are going to get. I got a higher standard of living."

When I first arrived, I barraged the Griers with tactless questions. Why did you create Whitestone Farms? And what are your religious beliefs? And why did you come to Alaska? Do you really share everything in common? How can people give up their privacy, their property? Do your children stay?

I knew better. I was violating the rules of field research. I had not established trust. I was asking too many questions, too many sensitive questions, too soon. The Griers and others at Whitestone Farms gave me answers, but it took me many years to understand their answers. I was a secular Jew, unfamiliar with Christian spiritual ideals. This religious community in Alaska was as strange to me as a tribe in Australia.

The Community's Origin Story

The origin of Whitestone Farms was a fantastic tale, the venture modeled upon a Biblical narrative. Whenever I asked someone at Whitestone what the community was about, why they had come to live on a desolate piece of land in the Alaska wilderness, thousands of miles from their families, every person referred to the same narrative, quoting the verse in Acts 4:32: "And the congregation of those who believed were of one heart and soul; and not one of them claimed that anything belonging to him was his own, but all things were common property to them." They lived out the Biblical plot and theme of Acts 4:34–35 in a literal way—selling their own land, houses, and businesses on the East Coast and combining the proceeds in this spiritual venture: "There was not a needy person among them, for all who were owners of land or houses would sell them and bring the proceeds of the sales and lay them at the apostles' feet, and they would be distributed to each as any had need."

The people who created Whitestone Farms had originally gathered around an old Congregational church in Claremont, New Hampshire, its graveyard dating back to the 1600s. Some lived in Claremont while others moved there, from such places as Keene, New Hampshire, and Martinsburg, Pennsylvania, in search of a serious spiritual life. One church member offered employment to other members of the fellowship. People from the church began to home school their children together, eat meals together, and help each other with household work.

When Bill Grier went to the Claremont group to preach, he found a church fellowship group getting closer and wanting to live together, to realize the Christian ideal in this world. He joined this group as their preacher. God was calling them to live together in community, they believed, and they named their congregation the Church of the Living Word. About a third of the church members felt that they could not live in such a communal society, and they separated from the rest—the event the community called in its origin narrative "The Great Sifting."

The Church of the Living Word started to search for land where they could live and work as one community. Nothing worked out in New Hampshire. Property deals fell through. Members of the church began to look farther away for land. Like the people who had founded so many other utopian communities in America, they found themselves drawn to the frontier. Large tracts of cheap land could be purchased in Alaska. Legal restrictions were minimal. Schooling their own children would not face the difficulties they had experienced in New Hampshire. Home schooling was commonplace in Alaska, where so many families lived in isolated mining areas, trapping cabins, and small, remote outposts. Alaska also offered the geographic isolation so important to creating their narrative of separation. Like the Pilgrims who journeyed to the New World, the people of Whitestone Farms wanted to raise their children apart, away from the seductions of the surrounding society.

In November 1981, the Claremont church sent three brothers to look at property in southeast Alaska. The men also looked over a broken-down homestead for sale in Delta Junction, a property recommended by another Christian communal society, Dry Creek, which had settled nearby. "The difference is like Sophia Loren and a plain, faithful wife," said Bill Grier. "The Southeast is more beautiful, but the Delta land will support us." Once the church started scouting for land, some members of the Claremont community liquidated their businesses so they could move quickly. They took factory jobs and odd jobs to bring in money. Some sold their homes and moved in with each other. They were getting ready for what the community named in its origin narrative the "Move of God."

The people created a daring plan. Some members of the congregation would go to Alaska and settle the land, constructing the Tabernacle and building housing for the community. Other members of the congregation would stay in Claremont, work for money, and send their earnings to church members in Alaska. The families who went to Alaska would rotate back to Claremont to take their turn earning money so others could go to Alaska. The plan required an extraordinary level of trust. People would be sending their earnings to people to whom they were not related, counting on them to return to take their places, trusting that dwellings would be built, the land would produce, and the communal society would succeed.

The incredible venture succeeded, and the Church of the Living Word was reunited in Alaska. When the last people from Claremont finally came to their promised land in Alaska, all the members of the community already there would be waiting for their crossing over the river. Sometimes they set off firecrackers. Nancy Porter described the reunion as "like I was meeting people who had died and now were alive."

The first group of nineteen pilgrims caravanned from New Hampshire to Alaska in a convoy of trucks and campers, traveling four thousand miles, and arriving on the George Probst Homestead on April 1, 1982. The temperature was thirty degrees below zero. Their dream land turned out to be nothing but a trailer with a two-story plywood addition with a dirt floor, made from the panels used to ship pipe for the Trans-Alaska Pipeline. The structure lacked insulation. Bill Grier had to be restrained from torching it. The pilgrims circled their campers and built a fire and began to build their community.

"Do you remember Squanto in the Pilgrims?" said one of the men to me. "The guy we bought our property from was a kind of Squanto. The first day we arrived, he went and made a fire in the stove for us. He kept our road plowed. He kept his house open. He let us make telephone calls. We had no idea how to farm, to make a garden in this land. We were going to use spades. Then we look up and he is coming over with a big tractor. We were too ignorant to know better. We just cried."

At their first Thanksgiving dinner, twenty-eight people crowded into the trailer. They had received a package from Claremont and people wondered what it contained—maybe a pumpkin cheesecake, the specialty of a brother at the Claremont church. "The gift was much more overwhelming," wrote Nancy Porter. "Everyone in the church had sent their most precious object: a treasured antique teapot, jewelry, clothing. People sent their life savings. The note enclosed said they wanted us to be able to stay on the land together and not have to be separated while some went out to work."

The people of Whitestone Farms saw their journey to Alaska as retracing the tale of the American founding. "The children presented a program that showed how the journey of the Pilgrims to their land paralleled in many ways the journey to our land," wrote Nancy Porter years later. "They read passages from journals of early settlers in Plymouth conveying their thankfulness at God's provision for them." William Bradford's entry for September 6, 1620, in his *History of Plymouth Plantation* describes a scene parallel to the experience of the pilgrims at Whitestone Farms: "And for the season it was winter, and they that know the winters of that country, know them to be sharp and violent. What could now sustain them but the Spirit of God and his grace?"

The first people to arrive at Whitestone Farms lived in the ramshackle plywood building attached to the trailer. They had no electricity, cut wood for heat, and used kerosene lamps for light. "Blanket City" they called their quarters because they hung blankets from the ceiling to create privacy for the couples. They used tape recorded music to create a sound barrier between the beds. When they said "good night" to each other, a wave of "good nights" rippled from one bed to another, embracing them in the heady emotion of shared purpose.

Their original plan was to build separate cabins for each family. But the experience of living together in one household was so exhilarating that they decided to build communal housing, each family having a bedroom in a common building. They hauled in their building materials over the ice road in winter and constructed the buildings as a community. Families lived together with each couple living in one bedroom and their small children having a bedroom nearby. Teenagers lived in different buildings.

They were building a city on a hill but they were also building an actual city. The community needed electricity, a system for water and waste disposal, and housing for the growing families. The community needed cash for medical and dental services, for the food they could not grow, and for building materials. The people worked long hours, on the farm and at their outside businesses, trying to find a balance between the need to make money to support the community and the need to maintain the ecstatic spiritual life that was the purpose of the community. During religious services, many members spoke in tongues, weddings featured a "covering" of the new couple with the elders of the church and their families making a canopy over them.

"This looks totally crazy from the world's point-of-view, what we're doing here," said Andy Hibshman, a secular Jew who had joined the community in Claremont and then had moved to Whitestone Farms. "We are doing something here that really has not been done too often in the world's history. To build a spiritual community from nothing. It's exciting to be part of something like this, from the beginning."

That's what he tried to tell his mother when she told him that living in the community was a "cop-out," that they were after his inheritance. Hibshman had his own spiritual doubts. "Personally if for some reason I am wrong and there is no God and our vision is wrong, I'm still glad I'm doing this. It is a great way of living," he said.

The Spiritual Frontier

I could not understand why educated, sane people would choose to live this way. Many were college graduates, a number were teachers, one was a journalist, and another was a vibrations engineer. "I never thought I would be a janitor," remarked Bill Grier, who worked in rotation with the other men of the community cleaning offices at night. "In my family, we were raised to be public servants, like police officers."

Cleaning out barns, cleaning the bathrooms, cooking meals for 180 people, baking pies, and serving food to the tourists at Rika's Road-house—such work was difficult and demanding. As I spent more time in the community, I began to understand other difficulties, the more subtle problems of living in a Christian community. You could express only positive, uplifting emotions. You had to see in the worst adversity, not tragedy, but the will of God. You had to develop a spiritual fortitude that I found unfathomable.

I could not understand Mary Baranoski's acceptance of the death of her husband, Stan, and her oldest son, seventeen-year-old Matthew, on June 30, 1994. Her husband and son were in a Piper PA-22, searching the silt-gray Tanana River for a lost riverboat when the engine sputtered and the small plane crashed. Mary Baranoski and her remaining two sons moved from their home at one of the community's businesses, the Tanana Trading Post, into a room at the school. "I'm convinced that what happened was not an accident," she declared, refusing to admit to a very normal human desire, the wish that such a disaster had not befallen her. "I'm convinced that it was God's will and purpose for their lives and for our lives and I'm certain that if they were given the choice to return, they would not return. Already they've been released to love us more fully and care for us more fully than they ever have. I don't want to go back."

The spiritual frontier—I had not known such a frontier even existed before I went to Whitestone Farms. In an article for the school news-paper, one teenager, Oshea Graf, discussed her personal spiritual tests with candor: "I live on a corporate farm and most often I can work and work and not be seen for the accomplishments I have made. This is very hard for me personally, because I am a human being who loves attention and basks in the light of all eyeballs looking at me." The students inter-preted what others would consider normal teenage behavior as spiritual struggles—trying to control their obsession with their appearance, trying to cut out the sarcastic remarks designed to put their peers in their place, the hurtful put-downs that Bill Grier called "honesty without truth."

Other spiritual issues demanded constant vigilance. At Whitestone Farms, people were expected to exercise constant forbearance and self-control. Every person was created in the image of God and deserved, there-fore, care and consideration. Dealing with the complaints of the irritable tourists who arrived in busload after busload at Rika's Roadhouse was interpreted as a test of the spirit. "A lot of people come through the park and they are self-centered and make demands. We say that we are here to serve these people. Go out and do your best with a smile on your face. We do it in love and care," said one of the people who worked at the restaurant. The people of Whitestone spent hours giving physical care and compan-ionship to an adult man in the community in a wheelchair, who was born with spina bifida and legally blind. The entire community learned a new method for stimulating the development of neurological pathways in the brain of a little girl at the farm born with Down syndrome so they could teach her constantly. "The success of Whitestone is in the fact that we see all people as desperately needy," wrote Nancy Porter. "Some disabilities are more obvious than others."

The need for such constant emotional control and concern for oth-ers left me exhausted whenever I returned from fieldwork. I understood why Whitestone Farms saw the community not as a "utopia" but rather as a "furnace of affliction." You would be corrected, kindly, but corrected nonetheless, when your appearance did not meet community standards or when you said something thoughtless.

Raising children in community brought spiritual tests people found the most difficult. Different families had different standards for the behavior of children, and no one liked other people correcting their chil-dren. "Bringing up children, that's where I have had to lay my will down, where I've been put to the test, to do what's best for the community," one elder told me. Conflicts over raising children had broken up other wilder-ness farms. At community meetings, people tried to set up common ex-pectations: Children should wait and not interrupt adults when they are talking. Adults could correct other people's children but only if the adult already had developed a personal relationship with the child. If someone in the community corrected a child, the parent should side with the adult in public and later discuss in private what had happened and whether the adult was justified in intervening.

Whitestone Farms had no constitution, no compact, no written rules or regulations. I asked an elder how the community could function in this fashion. What if one family wanted to take a trip back to the East Coast to visit their relatives, when the family's airplane tickets would cost the community thousands of dollars? What if some complained about having to live in the beaten-up homestead with its dirt floors while others got to live in the new housing with amenities like small kitchens and common rooms? The elders drew a distinction between a religion of law and a religion of the spirit: "The whole purpose of the church is to put you in communion with the Lord, not to put you under law. If we established rules, we would kill the very thing we were trying to create."

Most community decisions were made by elders who were not elected. People just knew when someone should be made an elder: "When people are hearing from the Lord, they are sensitive to other people. They are careful with other people. They are not grabbing for themselves." Some community decisions took place at family meetings of the whole community—like the debate on whether or not to get a dog. Luckily for the children, God wanted a dog.

Narrative Identity on the Spiritual Frontier

These seekers—what exactly were they searching for? And why were they willing to give up so much for it? And what in the end had they found? Few left Whitestone Farms. After six years, I took a census and found that eighty-five percent of the people I had met the first year were still living in Whitestone Farms or in other religious communities. The young people could choose whether to leave the community or to stay. Whitestone Farms had no special ceremony to mark the decision to join the community. People just knew when the children had made their choice.

The children faced a hard choice. Their parents had experienced the excitement of being part of a pioneering experience, the exhilaration of creating a new society in the wilderness. But the children took life in a communal society for granted. Emerson William Eads, the grandson of the founder, Bill Grier, had the gift of charisma. Emerson led the Whitestone choir and dreamed of becoming a famous conductor. Emerson had won the state oration contest and dreamed of becoming a lawyer and judge. When someone from outside the community asked him what he was doing with his life, should he tell them he was just a janitor? He was ashamed, he told me, well, not really ashamed. Yes, he was going to college but then he was going to Covenant Life College at the farm. I ached for him, I wanted for him the same career success I wanted for my own children. I also did not want this spiritual experiment to perish.

Emerson had been offered a debating scholarship to the University of Alaska. Should he take it? He prayed with the elders for guidance and they "sent for visions." Within the religious communities in the Alaska wilderness are believed to live people with prophetic gifts. When someone has a crucial decision to make, they are asked for visions for a man or a woman without specifying the nature of the dilemma. The visions arrived by fax. Emerson received a vision from someone in another religious community. The dream told of a man walking into a shoe store and seeing a row of gleaming dress shoes. At the end of the row was a pair of muddy boots that the man in the dream had put on. Emerson had just volunteered to clean the manure out of the pig barn, and his boots were muddy. As he interpreted the vision, he should wear the boots of Whitestone Farms. He stayed in the community, then left, rising quickly in the business world, and then returned to stay at Whitestone Farms.

The people of Whitestone Farms found it as hard to understand my family, secular Jews, as I was finding it to understand them. After my three teenage children spent time at the community, I received a delicate letter from Nancy Porter: "I hope the questions that were asked of them here were not offensive in any way. Because our Whitestone children have viewed the Old Testament from a Christian point of view, I think they found your children's lack of a personal relationship with God and no belief in an afterlife or the coming of the Messiah unique."

My children found the spiritual passions of the community equally unfathomable. "I've told a lot of people in New York about Whitestone," said my thirty-year-old son years later. "They can't believe such a place exists in the twenty-first century. What's so fascinating about them is that they're such ordinary down-home people, sane as anybody and more productive than most . . . except that they believe that an omniscient, omnipotent, invisible spirit told each of them personally to go to an island in the middle of nowhere."

As I recorded their life histories, I began to understand the life of the spirit that the people of Whitestone Farms were seeking. Richard Greenleaf, an elder, described this life and its conflicts with unusual clarity. At nineteen years of age, Greenleaf saw his life stretching out before him like a well-marked highway. He had grown up in a close, church-going family in a small Pennsylvania town. His father, a carpenter by trade, owned a construction business and he ("a giver") was planning to give the business to his two sons. Greenleaf had married his high-school sweetheart, and her father, a prosperous banker, had arranged for a bank loan so they could move right into a house of their own. They had it made.

But he and his wife were searching for something more. After a year of trying out different churches, they decided to try out the Church of the Living Word in Claremont, New Hampshire. They liked the people more and more as time went on. Twice a month, they would leave work on Friday and drive for nine hours to fellowship with the church in Claremont. Late Sunday night they would drive the nine hours back. The commuting was crazy.

"We felt that God wanted us to move to Claremont," said Greenleaf. They did, and within a year, his brother had joined him. They understood they were hurting their parents. If they had left for better jobs, their parents would have understood. But leaving for a church? Moving to be with people they didn't know at all well, with people their folks didn't know at all? Their parents worried about what their sons were getting themselves into, perhaps a cult. Richard Greenleaf understood what his family wanted for him in life but believed what his family wanted conflicted with what God wanted. He feared he was starting to do what his father had done, to work all the time. "If I hadn't made the break from my family, I wouldn't be so involved with the things of God. And this is really my life. It really is," he said.

What did it mean to be involved with things of God? I asked him for a concrete example. He told me about listening to children: "One of the eighth-grade boys called me yesterday and I'm awfully busy, and he wants to know where something is in the woodshop. I need to give him the same care and attention as if Bill Grier had called and wanted me to do something. That's the way we operate because God is no respecter of persons." In other words, God makes no distinctions between the leader of the community and the child.

I was starting to understand the spiritual frontier and the narrative identity the people of Whitestone Farms had created. I so often fail to listen, even to my own children. My mind is on my work or on the next task I have to accomplish. At Whitestone Farms, a person like me would be corrected. "You can't be so given to work, to a project, that you aren't taking care of people, honoring them and respecting them by giving them your full attention. We have a way of requiring, I won't say excellence, but a greater standard," Richard Greenleaf put it. "If a person isn't giving himself, people will talk to him about it. But you have to do it in care and love."

"I do the same thing in my relationship with my husband," I told Greenleaf. "If I am worried that something he is doing will hurt him, I tell him but, yes, in the spirit not of criticism but of care and love."

Greenleaf was pleased that I had finally understood what he had been trying to explain. He built on my metaphor. "This community is a lot like marriage," he said. "A marriage is a commitment. You have got to spend time together. You have got to communicate. You don't just fix what you like to eat. You don't just buy big things without talking to your own husband, do you? Just take what you are doing between you and your husband and make it on a bigger scale."

When I asked Richard Greenleaf my standard interview question— what the story of his life should say—he gave his answer more quickly than anyone else I had ever interviewed: "I want to be a godly man. I would want to be known as someone who cared more for the interests of others than for myself. I would want to be known as someone who did not just talk about that but whose life demonstrated that. To lose my life in a sense—my drive and my personal ambition—and to make sure that my life is really given in a way that will honor God and my fellow man."

"I hope I have not been a disappointment to my Dad," he added.

Whitestone Farms saw itself as a remnant, people who had turned their back on the world in an effort to live as the Lord wanted people to live. They were looking for more than a pristine environment, ecologically and morally, in which to raise their families. They were more than a group of believers who just liked to be together. They saw themselves as called out from the world into a spiritual community that shared a radical commitment to deny themselves and follow the Lord. They were struggling to eradicate the self-centeredness within. They were attempting to insulate themselves from the materialistic, competitive, self-absorbed lifestyles of people in the surrounding world, to the degree that they could.

Their separation contained an irony. When they went to Alaska, they became part of America's frontier romance, of the narrative of leaving the Old World to build a religious community in the wilderness. In Alaska, they were becoming more of a "light unto the world" than they ever had been in New Hampshire. In the summer of 1994 alone, sixty-one visitors came to Whitestone Farms, not only from the United States but also from countries like Ireland and South Africa. Few people had visited them in New Hampshire. Some visitors arrived suspicious, like state troopers who came to investigate or the tax examiners who came to check their books. But the visitors left impressed by these spiritual seekers.

The community made me reflect on the values I lived by, my fever for accomplishment, the narrative identity I had constructed as a frontier-woman who had accomplished far more by "going west, young woman" than she could ever have achieved had she stayed in the populated East. A peculiar thought kept forcing its way into my consciousness. Could God have called me—precisely because I was a secular Jew who found this community so strange—to tell the story of these Christian seekers in the wilderness?

The people of Whitestone Farms had created a narrative identity from the frontier romance and from the story of the early Christians who lived communally. They had re-created both stories in the wilderness of Alaska, using narrative to construct new lives.

Conclusion

We are all storytellers and we are the stories we tell.

—McAdams, Josselson, and Lieblich, *Identity and Story*

This inquiry has explored how shared cultural stories shape people's lives, and, in particular, how a powerful master narrative, America's frontier romance, seizes lives. I have described particularly vivid and dramatic examples of the frontier romance, people who go to Alaska, "The Last Frontier," to live literally as mountain men, pioneer women, homesteaders, and spiritual seekers building a city on a hill in the wilderness. America's frontier romance gives them not only plot lines to follow, characters to emulate, stage locations to find, and props to support their theater of the imagination. The frontier romance also creates the moral justification for leaving their families and homes, for seeking more than comfort and success. The story gives them courage to leave the familiar, take the risk, and set out on a road of tests and trials. The narrative creates a romantic illusion, coloring dangers and hardships in an alpenglow of blue mountains, silver rivers, and golden cabins. What is remarkable is how many succeed in actually "going west and rising with the country," in actually living in cabins in the wilderness, in actually living like nineteenth-century mountain men. Not only the hardships and dangers but also the beauty, accomplishments, and satisfactions are quite real. The illusion and the reality are inseparable. The romance midwifes the reality.

I have used people who go to Alaska to illustrate the way a master narrative seizes lives. But I do not want to end this inquiry leaving the impression that the frontier romance works its magic only in such extreme cases. The narrative can seize ordinary moments and serve as script for extraordinary actions. Let me illustrate how this can happen by a day in the life of a lawyer, an ordinary, respectable "suit." John Tiemessen is a major medical malpractice attorney, well-respected and well-liked in his community, a pillar of the community who has been president of the local bar association, the state bar association, and his Rotary club. Driving home with his daughter from an ordinary day at the office, an out-of-the-ordinary occurrence causes him to be seized by the frontier romance and he actually acts it out on the highway. The story grips his imagination and guides his actions. He even embellishes his drama with musical instrumentation and a musical score.

From the perspective of narrative psychology, for understanding how stories turn into life, what is important to recognize is that, yes, Tiemessen is enacting a story, but he is also acting, in the actual world. Had the frontier romance not been swirling through his imagination, John Tiemessen would not have gone out and gotten his gun. Nor would he have helped his neighbor.

> It's about as stereotypical a North Pole tale as I have experienced. *[Tiemessen begins with a feint. He pretends this will be a story about a place, about North Pole, Alaska—a northern Dogpatch in Alaska iconography, where people, like his neighbors, live in trailers still sitting on their axles and fill their yards with collections of broken-down machinery, snowmachines that won't run, and Trans Ams up on blocks. Pretending that this story is about a place, not a person, camouflages the central purpose of the story, which is the creation of an alternative, imaginative identity.]*
>
> Last night my daughter and I are driving home. About one-half mile from the house we see a small herd of pigs walking down a side street. We stop, yell "Sooooie" out the window, and finally decide to head home and call animal control. *[Calling the authorities is the conventional action an ordinary good citizen would take; the frontier romance has not yet taken hold.]*
>
> As we turn into our driveway, I see my neighbor walking around the yard, looking around. I ask her if she is missing her pigs. Now these are no ordinary pigs. These are Russian boars. Big, bristly tusked animals with large powerful heads and black hair. They look like they jumped off a European hunting tapestry. After recounting to me the tale of her no-good-abusive-sonofabitch husband who can't set foot

on their property because of a restraining order, she confirms that these pigs are missing. She thinks that her husband came to the house and let them out to get even for the restraining order. *[So begins the invitation to enter a story: a damsel is in distress and needs rescuing; the picturesque and picaresque pigs have evoked in the staid lawyer's imagination the heroic tales portrayed in medieval tapestries.]*

The Great North Pole Pig Roundup was on. *[The lawyer projects onto town and pigs the imagery of a cowboy town and a cattle roundup. But his tone is ironic; he is making fun of himself and his fascination with western imagery even as the narrative takes hold.]*

We headed down to where I had last spotted the elusive creatures and tracked them to their lair. This was pretty easy because there was a lot of grunting and squealing. The pigs were making a lot of noise too. We all got sticks, the preferred tool of most pig wranglers, and tried to herd them back to the house. *[In reality, the pigs are not hiding in a lair, the pigs are running around in plain sight near the highway. In reality, Tiemessen is not tracking them, he couldn't miss their grunting and squealing. His imagery links the runaway pigs with the heroic quest, tracking down monsters hiding in their lair. Calling himself a "pig wrangler," he again draws on cowboy imagery to create a frontier identity, the juxtaposition of "pig" and "wrangler" mocking his own playacting.]*

The boar, sow, and piglets took off and everyone took off after them like a cross between *Deliverance* and *Lord of the Flies.* You could almost hear the fast-picking banjo music from *Smokey and the Bandit* playing. *[New layers of heroic imagery from different genres of film and literature—tragedy, parable, and comedy—now embellish the narrative, as well as banjo music that adds to the picaresque quality of the tale.* Deliverance *is a 1972 tragedy telling the tale of a group of men embarking on a dangerous river rafting trip into the backcountry.* Lord of the Flies *is a 1954 novel by William Golding describing a group of boys who descend from civilization to savagery when their plane is shot down. In the opening scenes, the boys too are hunting wild pigs.* Smokey and the Bandit *is a 1977 comedy featuring a sheriff chasing a bandit hired to drive across county lines a truck filled with beer. Tiemessen is using a medley of images—masculine, savage, dangerous, and wild—to present himself as both hero and comic rogue.]*

We next tried a pig drive. I came up with the great idea of lasso-
ing the boar. When I got close, my neighbor warned, "The boar bites."
Eyeing his two-inch tusks, I abandoned my plans to wrangle the pig.
[Cowboy imagery again takes over the story line.]

At this point some of you might be wondering why I didn't go
home. I was under no obligation, moral or otherwise, to dispatch these
animals. But the boars were dangerous and I sure couldn't round them
up and drive them home. The answer is simple, you don't get many
opportunities to do something like this, and if there were going to be
shots fired into the neighborhood that night I wanted to be the one doing the shooting. *[By now caught up in the cowboy romance, Tiemessen is not going to back away from the challenge of getting these pigs.
He justifies his actions in the name of neighborhood safety but he is
caught up in the story of "Tiemessen the Cowboy," narrated in a self-
deprecating style as "Tiemessen the Comical" for reasons that become
clear later on, when we interpret this story together.]*

I went back to the house and tried to select the proper firearm
for the task. I decided that magnum hunting rifles were too much for
these beasts and that the .22 was a little on the light side. Handguns
were too risky a shot. I finally settled on a .30-caliber M1 Carbine with
a 30-round clip, just in case the pigs returned fire. *[The gun-toting
cowboy is not an entirely fictitious identity. This respected and respectable Alaska attorney owns a collection of guns that he uses for
the occasional hunting trip, for bear protection at his cabin, and to
establish and embellish his imaginative identity as a self-sufficient
woodsman.]*

I dispatched the beasts from just beyond the roadside. One nice
thing about North Pole is that no one calls the cops or even slows
down when they see a man standing on a busy street and shooting into
the ditch with an assault rifle at 11:15 at night. *[Reality and romance
unite. Alaska is still a frontier culture, reminiscent of the Wild West.
In Alaska, no one finds the sight of a man shooting a gun at pigs in a
ditch a spectacle worthy of slowing down, let alone calling the police.*

*While Tiemessen had planned to drop the "pile of porkchops" in
his neighbor's yard, on the hood of her broken-down '77 Trans Am,
her two boys shirk the work, insisting they don't "know nothing 'bout
guttin' no pigs." The lawyer goes home, gets his hunting knives, guts
the pigs, and hangs the carcasses in game bags on chains in the yard.*

Tiemessen owns hunting knives and game bags, and, he is telling us, has the competence of an expert woodsman to gut and hang the animals he shoots. He stumbles home bloody and greasy at 1:30 a.m. Figuring only his dog could stand the smell of him, he showers and falls into bed.]

The story about the "Great North Pole Pig Roundup," which takes place in a few hours one summer evening, purports to be a story about a Dog-patch of a place, North Pole, Alaska, where people keep Russian boars, where people's yards are filled with broken equipment (always handy should they need a spare part), and where domestic battles create daily drama. But the story, like virtually all the stories we tell about our lives, is not about a place but about a person. The theme of the life story is what kind of people we are. John Tiemessen may look like a "suit," but he is Clark Kent in disguise, the kind of man who helps a woman in distress, the kind of man who does not dial 911.

His life history interview reveals the psychological functions the story serves in creating both his inner and public identity. The "Great North Pole Pig Roundup," Tiemessen realizes as we unpack its themes and imagery, is a story that "lets me publicize myself without bragging." Tiemessen is short in stature, a smart boy, who used his wit and talent for comedy to secure his standing among the boys at school. As his life story unfolds, he describes his admiration for his manly, competent father ("my dad was a big deal") and the pleasure he takes in the "deep play" of going out alone on weekends to his wilderness cabin, chopping wood and fixing up the cabin. In his play as a woodsman living in a cabin, he is imitating Dick Proenneke, a wilderness dweller who starred in a film he made about himself. Proenneke set up a movie camera and filmed himself building alone a cabin in the forest, beginning with cutting and peeling the logs and ending with bringing in stones for a great rock fireplace. His website contains the lines:

Thousands have had such dreams,
but Dick Proenneke lived them.
He found a place, built a cabin, and
stayed to become part of the country.

John Tiemessen, the "Great North Pole Pig Roundup" communicates, is quite a man, like Dick Proenneke. Tiemessen can choose and use guns and hunting knives, can dispatch dangerous and wild animals, gut them without assistance, and hang up the carcasses on chains. John Tiemessen, the story is intended to tell us, is not only a manly man, but also a good man, the kind of man who helps out his neighbors, even when it costs him sleep, heavy work, and trouble, even when his neighbors have brought their problems upon themselves through their domestic warfare.

This story of "the lawyer as cowboy," together with the stories of the mountain men, pioneer women, and utopian seekers, which unfold over many years, illustrates the ways in which cultural narratives like the frontier romance shape lives.

1. Master narratives drive action by offering characters to emulate, scenes to play, costumes to wear, props to hold, values to uphold, and poses to strike.

While narrative psychology has rightly stressed the function of narrative in creating the life story, a coherent, unified sense of self, narratives also create action in the actual world. For many of those who migrated to Alaska, the decision to go to what they saw as a "frontier" was a central life transition and turning point in their lives. The frontier romance guided the settings in which they chose to live, the clothes they chose to wear, the log houses they chose to build or buy, and the plots and values they lived by. The master narrative functions not like a blueprint for a building but more like the lush illustrations in a travel guide, filled with romantic pictures and poses, stock scenes and scenery.

2. Master narratives create realities, weaving together the stories in people's minds and the settings they find.

As narrative psychologists realize, the story and the actuality create each other. For those who choose to live the frontier romance in Alaska, the narrative creates the psychological "set"—images and expectations they bring to the setting. The narrative makes them search out and see the opportunities in an unsettled, turbulent society and encourages them to ignore the ordinariness of actual Alaska cities and the difficulties of life in a remote region. The narrative encourages people to put themselves in situations—remote towns off the road system without power and plumbing, cabins in the woods, communities in the wilderness—that support their story of themselves. The narrative encourages them to surround themselves with symbols that support their imaginative conception of Alaska—log cabins and Carhartts, gun collections and gold dredges. They choose to see and to stress those features of the actual environment that serve the romance and to ignore features in conflict with the story.

3. A master cultural narrative can serve different psychological functions for different individuals.

The frontier narrative typically supports ambition, giving people the courage to leave the security of home and head for a new world where they can create a better world. This is the theme Horace Greeley encapsulates in his exhortation to "go west, young man, and grow up with the country." The self-help shelf draws on this quintessential American theme, urging people to explore new worlds, to take the risk, to have the courage to go beyond their comfort zones, assuring them that they will be sufficient. But the frontier narrative can be turned to many diverse purposes, and this inquiry, despite its narrowness of scope to Alaska frontier dwellers, reveals many of them:

- Pursuing conventional ambition or rebelling from such ambition
- Seeking redemption and rebirth
- Proving up as a man
- Providing dignity to people who would otherwise regard themselves as failures
- Healing and camouflaging psychological disturbance
- Creating a new and more perfect society

The frontier narrative drives what John Stuart Mill calls in his essay *On Liberty* "experiments of living."[1] Such experiments of living, Mill argues, benefit society in the same ways as freedom of speech. They offer to their audience diverse models of the good life, from which individuals can choose those that fit them best. Such experiments of living also make human life "rich, diversified and animating." The frontier romance similarly provides interesting theater for its audience.

Those Alaskans who live out the frontier narrative literally as mountain men, pioneer women, or pilgrims reassure the rest of us that our collective American narrative is alive and well: Our cherished story about our origins and ourselves is still true.

4. Communities, as well as individuals, use master narratives to create storied worlds.

Narrative psychologists understandably stress the importance of story as a way that individuals make sense of their lives and the importance of narrative therapy to counselors. Therapists use narrative to help individuals and families rewrite the scripts they are stuck in and author new story lines that, they hope, will lead to more fulfilling lives. The therapeutic goal may be to turn a victim story, for example, into a story of transcending tragedy, turning the errors of the past into lessons for the future, to underscore the need for taking control and moving forward.

A contribution of this study is to show how communities too use master narratives to display the values they stand for and to unite their members in shared purposes and understandings. The women of Central wove an identity of their small town at the end of the road as an early American pioneer community. They remind us of the neighborliness and mutual aid that we continue to believe should define American life. Whitestone Farms wove the story of itself as a communal society living out the story of the early Church and of journey to the frontier, defining itself in accordance with the ideals of sharing with each other and caring for each other without respect to ability, status, or social position.

In American society, the frontier romance provides cultural scaffolding that enables people to use freedom to construct who they will be. The love of freedom is far from natural. Freedom brings insecurity and anxieties, the burden of choice, the responsibility for making wrong choices, the prospect of failure, loneliness, and disillusionment. America's frontier narrative glamorizes freedom, attaching to the idea of freedom the beauty and grandeur of the West and its code of heroic honor.

Those who go to Alaska to live frontier lives are seeking and bearing witness to the freedom America offers. The mountain men, the pioneer women, and even those disturbed people who retreat into the wilderness as a strategy of coping with mental illness, say clearly, over and over again, that they are making these life choices in the name of freedom. They see themselves as bearing witness to the values America represents. They see themselves as sending a rejuvenating message to American society. All of us can escape from conventions we do not like, from roles that do not fit, from values we do not want to live by. We too can use freedom to forge our own lives and create new life stories.

Notes

Introduction: How Literature Turns into Life

1. Gerald D. Nash, *Creating the West: Historical Interpretations, 1890–1990* (Albuquerque: University of New Mexico Press, 1991), 208.
2. Frederick Jackson Turner, *The Frontier in American History* (1921; repr., Tucson: University of Arizona Press, 1986), p. 37.
3. John M. Faragher, *Rereading Frederick Jackson Turner* (New Haven, Conn.: Yale University Press, 1994), p. 1.
4. See, for example, Patricia N. Limerick, *The Legacy of Conflict: The Unbroken Past of the American West* (New York: W. W. Norton, 1988), and Nathan Glazer, "American Epic: Then and Now," *The Public Interest* 130 (Winter 1998). Glazer argues that this frontier epic was the dominant story of America through the 1940s but has been eclipsed by a second and quite different epic of America that emphasizes American misdeeds and "celebrates quite different voyages: the middle passage, the Trail of Tears, the immigrant ship, the underground railway, the tenement trail from slum to suburb." Note, however, that even such examples of the negative epic as the "underground railway, the tenement trail from slum to suburb" can also be read as triumphal images.
5. Joseph Campbell, *The Hero with a Thousand Faces* (1949, repr., Princeton, N.J.: Princeton University Press [Bollingen Series], 2008), p. 5. See also Shirley Park Lowry, *Familiar Mysteries: The Truth in Myth* (New York: Oxford University Press, 1982).
6. Lowry, *Familiar Mysteries.*
7. Nathan Glazer, "American Epic," pp. 7, 8.
8. John T. Juricek, "American Usage of the Word "Frontier" from Colonial Times to Frederick Jackson Turner," *Proceedings of the American Philosophical Society* 110 (1966): 10–34. Juricek locates the change in meaning in the mid-nineteenth century, stating: "Until at least the second third of the

nineteenth century, when Americans talked about frontiers, they habitually showed their preoccupation with defending them, not advancing them."

9. Erich Fromm, *Escape from Freedom* (New York: Henry Holt, 1941), p. 20.

10. George Wilson Pierson, *Tocqueville in America* (Baltimore: John Hopkins Press, 1948), 314–49.

11. Ibid., 334.

12. Ibid., 334.

13. Barry Schwartz, "Self-determination: The Tyranny of Freedom," *American Psychologist* 55 (2000): 79–88.

14. Fromm, *Escape from Freedom*.

15. Ibid., xiii.

16. Ibid., 48.

17. John McPhee, *Coming into the Country* (1977; repr. New York: The Noonday Press, 1991).

18. Alaska Humanities Forum, "Alaska 20–20" (Anchorage: Craciun Research Group, 2002).

19. Dan P. McAdams, Ruthellen Josselson, and Amia Lieblich, *Identity and Story: Creating Self in Narrative* (Washington, D.C.: American Psychological Association, 2006); Dan P. McAdams, *The Redemptive Self: Stories Americans Live By* (Oxford: Oxford University Press, 2005); George C. Rosenwald and Richard L. Ochberg, eds., *Storied Lives* (New Haven, Conn.: Yale University Press, 1992); Amia Lieblich, Dan P. McAdams, and Ruthellen Josselson, *Healing Plots: The Narrative Basis of Psychotherapy* (Washington, D.C.: American Psychological Association, 2004).

20. McAdams, *The Redemptive Self*.

21. I use in my discussion below Joseph Campbell's framework of the hero's journey. See Joseph Campbell, *The Hero with a Thousand Faces*.

22. Richard Hofstadter, *The Progressive Historians* (Chicago: University of Chicago Press, 1968), 67.

Chapter 1. Modern-Day Mountain Men

1. The description of Richard Gardner and Chris Batin was written by Batin for this book.

Chapter 2. The Pioneer Women

1. Jennifer Brice, *The Last Settlers* (Pittsburgh: Duquesne University Press, 1998).
2. J. S. Kleinfeld, "A Woman in Search of a Character: Adult Development in the Alaskan North," *Northern Review* 15/16 (winter 1995/summer 1996): 22–41.
3. Laurel Tyrrell, "Living Out the Frontier Myth in the Twenty-First Century" (master's thesis, University of Alaska Fairbanks, 2002), 57.
4. Jacqueline Wiersma, "The Press Release: Symbolic Communication in Life History Interviewing," *Journal of Personality* 56 (1988): 205–38.
5. This story comes from a collection of oral histories that Laurel Tyrrell collected in an unpublished manuscript, "Central: Stories of a Place." Such local narratives, Tyrrell points out, were told (1) to pass on wilderness skills and (2) to communicate the social norms of the community, such as the fine line between relying on others for assistance in wilderness emergencies and relying on one's self.
6. Pam Haskin and Laurel Tyrrell were compensated as research assistants and conducted the tape-recorded life history interviews in the women's homes. Since there is always an audience for a life history, there is no single "true story" that exists apart from context and audience. Nonetheless, as an outside researcher, I was easy to deceive with one-dimensional heroic tales when the women could mug for the camera. Women within the community knew enough about each other's lives to elicit other versions of their life histories that included problematic pasts, tragedies, and ambiguities of interpretation, such as the women's own doubts about what they were doing.
7. McAdams, *The Redemptive Self.*
8. Judy Ferguson, *Blue Hills* (Big Delta, Alaska: Glas Publishing, 2003).

Chapter 3. The Frontier Romance as Mask

1. In the ten years I have conducted this research, I have come across no woman who appropriated the frontier identity as a mask for psychological disorder. The tough and independent mountain man is a role that appeals to disordered men who cannot find a satisfying and productive masculine identity.

2. John E. Cawte, "Flight into the Wilderness as a Psychiatric Syndrome," *Psychiatry: Journal for the Study of Interpersonal Processes* 30 (1967): 149–61.

3. I suspect one reason many people avoid the frame of mental illness is that this label destroys the romance and undercuts the "everyman" quality of the quest narrative. Thus, Chris McCandless would not have been a satisfying hero in Jon Krakauer's bestseller *Into the Wild* if he were viewed as suffering from mental illness. Whether or not he was is a debatable issue.

4. I have been unable to locate western historiography that places these odd characters in a broader historical context. Perhaps these misfits have claimed the attention of folklorists more than historians because their individual melodramas are unimportant in histories of the westward migration.

5. The story of Nimrod comes from Elva R. Scott, *Jewel on the Yukon: Eagle City* (Eagle, Alaska: Eagle Historical Society & Museums, 1977).

6. Audrey E. Parker, *Livengood: The Last Stampede* (Tucson, Ariz.: Hats Off Books, 2003), 111–12.

7. Ibid., 112. The description is written in 1962 by Rob Foster but Foster does not give the year Billy Gates reentered society. He spent his old age in the Pioneer Home of Sitka, Alaska, telling the other old people about pioneering and people like himself, the "true prospectors."

8. This account comes from Tom Brennan, *Murder at 40 Below: True Crime Stories from Alaska* (Seattle: Epicenter Press, 2001). I have drawn as well from newspaper articles published about the case.

9. Such disturbances in the sense of smell is a symptom of schizophrenia.

Chapter 4. The Pioneers of the Spirit

1. Otto F. Kraushaar, ed., *Utopias: The American Experience* (Metuchen, N.J.: Scarecrow Press, 1980).

2. Arthur Bestor, *Backwoods Utopias. The Sectarian and Owenite Phases of Communitarian Socialism in America: 1663–1829* (Philadelphia: University of Pennsylvania Press, 1950). For a broader view of these societies, see Robert S. Fogarty, *American Utopianism* (Itasca, Ill.: F. E. Peacock, 1972).

Conclusion

1. John Stuart Mill, *On Liberty* (1859; repr., Indianapolis: Hackett Publishing, 1978), 60.

Index